Liberty for All,

Liberty and Justice or Death

By

Bruce Logan

1stBooks - rev. 6/19/01

Liberty for All,
Liberty and Justice or Death

This is a philosophical profile of the USA, discussing the deteriorization of morality and the problems arising therefrom. Included is a warning of the destruction we are bringing upon ourselves and our nation if we do not turn from our decadence. Included with the author's view of the future of our nation is the information needed for the salvation of those who will choose it at the hour of destruction.

The book begins with ten short essays that were written before the author decided to amplify them into a book. Following the essays are some true horror stories of attempts by our government or its agencies to destroy various US citizens. Attempt is made to very briefly explain the need for the morally strong to band together in a united effort to re-establish liberty. Some prophecies are cited to show that the re-establishing of freedom will be done concurrently with the predicted gathering of Israel.

ACKNOWLEDGMENTS

Various friends and family helped with preparation of this work. The author knows now what other writers mean when they say that their work would not be possible without their "helpers".

Brothers John L. And Joseph V. and son Aaron G., read the manuscript as it progressed, making valuable suggestions. Robert Simon helped immeasurably with suggestions for verbiage and also assisted greatly with his computer skills. Mother Margaret Lyman, and daughter Heidi, helped a great deal with editing, spelling and grammar.

Final draft review was done by historian, Tom Liddiard. He not only made mechanical corrections: spelling, grammar and punctuation, but he also corrected some errors in content. The author's confidence in the veracity of this work is due in large part to his respect for Tom's intellect and his considerable assistance.

Final editing of grammar, spelling and punctuation were done by Linda Wright. She worked unselfishly and hard with her considerable skills to clean up the author's errors. She is greatly appreciated.

FORWARD

The following pages will speak for themselves. They are certain to stimulate much criticism. The author, of course, is unconcerned about criticism unless it is justified. He has attempted to describe truthfully, the condition of his nation. Presented also are the actions needed for salvation of all who prefer peace and security for their families, rather than death and destruction.

Please forgive redundancy. The author has attempted to repeat himself on basic truths, hoping they might sink in.

Writing helps one to organize and consolidate one's own thoughts, concepts and beliefs. Through this process, attitudes must change somewhat, especially through study for backup evidence. Intensive thought, coupled with prayerful study, will certainly stimulate growth and maturity for one's personal philosophy.

The first chapter is a series of unpublished essays begun in 1993. From the time the ten essays (chapter one) were written till this book was finished, the author's opinion changed somewhat. The question of whether our nation can be brought back to acceptable levels of morality for survival was for him resolved. This is explained so that the reader can understand what might otherwise be considered to be inconsistency.

Certain "helpers" as described in the "acknowledgments" read and made suggestions for this thesis. One criticism was that the writer's style, the use of irony or facetiousness, might be misunderstood by some. Heaven forbid! Being misunderstood has plagued the author throughout his life. To avoid misunderstandings, underlined italics are used to show that the opposite to what is said is meant. Example: the word _Glorious_ when found thus (_italics_) means the opposite (rotten or detestable). If the author missed changing some of these, he apologizes and hopes the readers will catch the meaning without his aid.

Bold printing has been used for emphasis. When it is found in quotes, please remember that the emphasis is the author's. Instead of quotation marks,("—") quotes are italicized. When underlining occurs within italicized quotes, it was found that way in the writing being quoted. A very little paraphrasing has been done. Rather than give the idea that the author is taking credit for this verbiage, he has italicized it as quotes. The paraphrasing is so close to actual quotes that meanings have not been changed.

Natural law is much referred to thought these writings. **Natural law** means simply, that which is, truth unchangeable, scientific fact. Examples: what goes up must come down; to every action there is an equal and opposite reaction, an unchangeable phenomenon which probably cannot be altered even by God.

This book describes negative aspects of our nation's condition because they are there. Please don't get caught up in the negative, but look towards the end of the book for answers to overcoming and surviving the coming crisis. The **God of Israel** is fulfilling the promises He made to our fathers. Those of us who cannot see the reality of our present condition will probably fail to recognize the salvation that will be provided. The sole purpose of this **voice of warning** is to show Israel that there will be **salvation for those who will take it.**

CONTENTS

Chapter 6 is a short chapter about the horrible IRS Gestapo.

Chapter 7 tells the reader that the problems facing us will be corrected and that a new society will emerge with our freedom regained. A brief description is given of the Israelites and why God withdrew from them while promising to one day gather them again. The USA is termed Babylon. The reader is asked not to worry whether the Messiah will be Christ or another. This chapter reiterates that great destructions are coming and our only hope is in the **Perfect Law of Liberty** (the Ten Commandments) and that a place of gathering will be established for those who accept this (**God's law**). More is given about the coming revolution and subsequent rebuilding of our land, stronger and better. Advice is given not to take part in the carnage of the revolution. A little is given about the beauty of the new society.

Chapter 8 states that most don't want to hear negativity, and states that we must face the truth if we are to deal with it. The reader is asked not to look down on the less fortunate. A great dispensation of **God's** mercy is predicted. A parable is given showing how our government interferes with parenting of children. An anonymous document is presented advising us to be prayerful about that which we accept as truth. A final call is made for the reader to watch for destructions and be prepared to gather and help rebuild our free society. Some biblical scripture is quoted.

Chapter 9 gives brief description of how the new society will operate. Reiterates that Israel will gather as Babylon is being destroyed. Tells the reader to watch for the gathering and to join it. Anonymous treatise, *The coming Crisis and how to meet it* is quoted. The prophet Jeremiah is quoted.

CHAPTER 1

Essay 1

A series of essays are underway to explain the basis upon which the American people could save themselves and our nation as we know it. We present the proposition that if the decadence continues and expands we must fall.

The media is called upon to present our declaration to the people. It will not be popular. It will be controversial, angering and stimulating many to hatred. We will speak plainly, pulling no punches. Those caught up in abominations will, for the most part, refuse the truth and become our bitter enemies.

We seek the few who may listen, to tell them there is hope for any who will cease to adulterate themselves and who will resolve to become responsible for their own actions. We are non-sectarian, but invite participation by all, whether affiliated with religious groups or not. The human family is endowed with instinctive conscience and with powers of discernment. It helps us, though, to have choices presented. Those of the media who will help present these choices can take pride in the knowledge that they have served their nation well. Those with a sense of honor will feel duty-bound to assist this effort.

The topics to be discussed in these essays are principles already understood by many. These principles are taught in some circles. The "media" can help reach everyone. All in our nation should know that some are standing firmly on the side of morality. All should be told that allies for decency are sought after.

We hope ministers from all faiths will join with us in this effort, but our move is not of an evangelical nature. It is based on the premise that natural law, "cause and effect", demands a certain level of morality below which we cannot conduct ourselves without devastating results. Our goal is to stimulate men of all faiths and those without affiliations to gravitate towards natural life-saving principles which will have the result of creating a free orderly society, or **"Liberty and Justice for All"**.

Our treatise will present various aspects of our present social attitudes and actions, relating them to natural law. We will attempt to explain why we must accept proper principles and enact or re-establish proper laws or **perish.**

We accept the premise that men are endowed with high intellect and the ability to choose between good and evil. We observe a condition of our times

1

wherein all manner of enticements and choices, good and bad, are before all men. We understand that only those who because of a **desire** to be so, are reasonably clean. Only these will have the ability to think clearly enough to recognize and accept the truth. We petition our fellow men to take the time to meditate upon themselves and the condition of our nation. We challenge all to make a conscious, enlightened decision as to what we want for ourselves and our families. Do we want liberty through law, or the whoremongering, child molesting, human-sacrificing society we've become.

If the religious groups will join with us, so much the better. The code of conduct required is the "old time" foundation of most of them. We care not from whence comes the stimulus towards decency. We find it a worthy endeavor to call the nation's attention to the following fact: natural law demands a higher level of conduct than is practiced by the majority in this society. Not only must we conduct ourselves morally, but we must also demand decency from our associates. We cannot require love from our fellow man. We can, and must, demand respect for our **"rights"** and the **"rights"** of all **law abiding** citizens. Only if we are willing to defend our neighbor's **"rights"**, do we deserve protection of our own. Only if we are willing to defend each other against crime, can we be free from it.

Those who take these things lightly will suffer for it. One example is cited here to show the vein of the future essays: Child molesters have **no right** to life. They should be quickly stamped out to protect our society. This is only half of it. Those who will tolerate child molesters have **no right** to life either. If we will knowingly allow crime to take place, we deserve the same penalty as does the perpetrator. We become accessories to crime, both through our tolerance of it and by our lack of willingness to defend or protect the innocent among us.

Don't take this lightly. Join with us in this effort. Help present to the nation the proposition that we must return to a decent standard of morality or we will **surely perish**.

end of Essay 1

Essay No. 2

I am compelled to cry out to my **dying world**. We could stop our suicide. We probably won't. Surely at least a portion of this great society must have enough remaining intellect, morality and courage, that they might save themselves.

We are an educated nation. We can't claim ignorance of the world's historical lessons. All societies, when ripe with corruption, have been destroyed either from without or within. We will not be different. Thinking men with any semblance of decency must see what's happening to us and must make some effort to stem the tide.

Today, any man who speaks out against immorality subjects himself to ridicule or worse from most of his contemporaries. In tomorrow's world, history will have again followed its inevitable pattern. A small portion of our numbers will be rebuilding our society. Those who remain will be the strong, that small segment who have maintained moral courage and discipline over themselves enough so, that they will have developed the strength which will enable them to withstand the enticements to self-gratification, so popular and so prevalent today, and so debilitating to mankind.

The series of intended essays will anger many. This small voice hopes to stimulate a few to take stock of themselves and to start making choices on the side of **survival**. If this happens, hated opposition will rise simultaneously. In nature, all things have opposites. If a seed of good is planted, evil will surely rise to surround it. If these writings anger many, it will have to follow that some will also be stimulated to strengthen their resolve toward morality.

The author subscribes to no religious organization. Analogies are made on a basis of whether tenets, actions, policies, or laws have natural results which impact the well-being of society. No disrespect is meant for the various religions. They seem, for the most part, to teach some morality, which is mankind's only salvation. The churches, however, bicker amongst themselves and show great intolerance for any deviation from their particular concepts; so much so, that many of us are turned off by them. Church groups also tend to politicize themselves, or in other words, compromise their principles for whatever becomes popular within their own ranks.

Most church or religious organizations seem to do good primarily because most of the laymen participate from a desire to do good. The laymen want morality for themselves and their loved ones. Most church "hierarchies" are well

3

paid and have achieved power over the minds of parishioners. The statement that "absolute power corrupts absolutely" is **absolutely true.** No man can achieve power and remain humble unless he is a truly **God**-like man. There have been very few such men on this earth. The result is that vast numbers of parishioners wanting to follow righteous leaders are **blindly led** by greedy, politicized, proud power mongers.

It is probable that some religious leaders sincerely try to lead their flocks righteously. This must be difficult though, because it is not possible for any man to be uncorrupted by power. Religious leaders have systematically relaxed the standards of morality to more closely match the desires of the masses. Our nation is now a mixture of people with watered-down concepts of morality and some with total lack of it. We have many with diabolically anti-moral attitudes. We probably have a small number of very honorable, moral people. In general, we qualify for the title of a decadent people.

The foregoing is meant as an indictment against **only** that portion of organized religion that **merits** criticism. Those in this society who have moral character certainly come largely from the various religious denominations. Some may even be among the leadership. We are a decadent nation. Hopefully, the decent, moral individuals number in the thousands or even millions.

If the decadence continues to grow, which is probable, this nation will soon be in total anarchy. The government will cease to exist. The entitlements many hold onto so dearly will be only a memory. There will be no government, no assistance for the poverty-stricken, no social security. In danger of starvation, the masses will steal and murder, trying to survive. Those who have life-sustaining goods will find it necessary to kill those who try to take their goods from them. The killing and burning will raise a stench to the heavens. This entire land will mirror and magnify the Los Angeles riots. Few will escape. Blood will flow freely throughout the land. Only the very strong and the few honorable, moral individuals will have the courage to avoid the carnage. They will probably seek each other out. They will probably manage somehow, to gather out of the battleground to avoid having to kill to survive.

Moral, honorable men must, as a part of their morality, be involved in service to their fellow men. A part of this service must be an attempt to teach, or at least hold up a standard of conduct, the standard which must be adhered to if the race of man is to survive. At this point in history, if a standard is raised and if enough people will rally and clean up our society, we can survive and prosper. This possibility has always been and will always be. Sadly, my prophecy is that the adversary of right has too strong a foot hold. There won't be enough of a rally.

Corruption will continue and amplify. Men of honor, not wanting to participate in the carnage, will find or establish gathering places and wait out the destruction.

It is heartbreaking and horrible to visualize the annihilation of a nation such as ours. It is at the same time, wonderful to contemplate a society made up of the strong, honorably moral individuals from all over this land. They will build a new vibrant society, free of crime, a society wherein the multitudes won't feed off the production of the few. In this society, children will be able to grow up free from molestation from their own fathers and mothers.

This society will not be allowed to teach children that immorality is alright; alright because methods have been devised to partially protect them against the natural, devastating results of promiscuity and other crimes. In other words, teaching them immorality, which is one of the very most damaging of the many destructive principles being taught. The end of our society as we know it is imminent. A new and wonderful world will emerge. The laws of nature cannot be altered. There must be opposites in all things. Some good will arise from the evil.

All men are called upon to make a stand. All who qualify must begin to come forth with the might of right and make the choice for morality on a personal level, then they can be a light unto others. Those who qualify must disseminate their light so that all may see both strength and weakness. All may then make their choice, having seen both sides.

The ensuing essays will discuss various aspects of morality, or the lack of it, which have infiltrated our society to seal its doom. Participation is invited from all who are willing. Fear not the mistakes you will make in attempting to promote the right. A firm law of nature is that we all have the spirit of discernment according to our level of cleanliness. Anyone willing to proclaim the truth and present the facts about our decline will find himself or herself belittled. Evil will rise up in opposition. The honest in heart though, will listen, understand, and will resolve to maintain their honor.

Fear not the revulsion you may suffer for the sake of decency. Ten strong men can conquer a thousand weak ones. Study the forthcoming essays, write essays, discuss with your contemporaries the principles of decency necessary to the survival of mankind. On this basis, at the very least, many will gather out before the masses self-destruct. How wonderful if a revival of decency could be strong enough to save our nation. The choices are limited. Be strong enough to save yourself or perish. Make your choice.

end of Essay 2

Essay 3

Laws of nature give us hope that mankind has the ability to survive our suicidal tendencies. Some of these tendencies will be discussed with the expectation that most readers will be antagonized. Some, though, will be honest with themselves. They'll understand that whether these things go against desires or popular concepts has no bearing on their validity. The honest in heart have the ability to see truth even if it contradicts their own experiences or wants.

We have before us all manner of enticements. There are myriad viewpoints to the effect that as a free people we needn't restrain ourselves. Freedom is a wonderful thing, but sadly misunderstood. It must allow us to do all that we desire, except to infringe on the rights of others. Freedom of speech is a right most of us would fight for even unto death. Slander of another, however, oversteps the legitimate bounds of free speech. We have no right to tell a lie which will harm any individual or our society. We have no right to teach false principles which can harm individuals or our society. Under the guise of free speech, harmful practices are often espoused which cause damage. We have a societal obligation to stop such espousals. Is this understood? Any action which produces damaging, negative results must be classified as contrary to the natural laws of survival. Such action must be declared illegal.

Government's only legitimate function is the protection of society; protection against foreign powers and protection within of the law abiding citizens from the criminals. When government fails to protect its citizens, the natural result is that they lose respect for government and for its laws as well. A government must not establish laws which cause or allow infringements on the rights of its citizens; when it does, the process of self-destruction has begun.

We live in a world wherein a lack of self-discipline abounds. This has resulted both from our self-created permissive environment and from genetic deterioration. We breed our animals for desired characteristics. It is seldom, indeed, that we seek our own mate on other than physical attraction and seldom with real knowledge about his or her character. If persons with great moral courage would seek each other for procreation, we would, in a few generations, have a great many courageous, moral giants. For the most part we have taken the opposite road. Weakness is created the same way as is strength. Uniting with persons who have the same weaknesses as our own will produce offspring with a magnification of those weaknesses. This is prominent among reasons for legally forbidding incest and marriages among close cousins. Laws forbidding such have long been in effect throughout this land. It is doubtful that today's permissive society would enforce these laws which are designed strictly for the good and strength of us all and the well-being of our society.

If you would develop a strong-muscled physique, the procedure is simple—good diet and exercise. The procedure for developing a musical talent is similar. You must practice your music. Intellectual development does not happen without study, without intellectual exercise. Be honest with yourself. Can you develop self-discipline without exercising the same? Constant, regular exercise will develop all our abilities. A lack of exercise will not. If we practice foregoing self-discipline, go against our teachings and conscience whenever the desire strikes us, we soon will have no ability to discipline ourselves.

In basic training, years ago, the U.S. Army taught us to obey all commands without question. We were informed that it might become necessary for a commander to order his troops to certain death, this, for the overall good of a battle's outcome. Military theory at that time was to the effect that a commander whose troops lacked the discipline to carry out orders could not win wars. It was believed that these men were therefore unfit, or of no value to the military forces of the United States of America. The theory was correct then and still is.

Self-discipline is the basis of individual morality. Without self-regimentation there is no morality. We've experienced a gradual weakening of our moral standard. This has brought the world and our nation to a position wherein many are genetic misfits. Many others are self-created deviates from morality. Normal humans have natural, proper desires towards procreation, self betterment, social acceptance, economic well-being and intellectual prowess. These pursuits are healthy under conditions of morality. They can cause self and societal destruction if not controlled. An uncontrolled desire for economic well-being generally turns to greed and covetousness. This usually leads to ignoring fair play and often to theft, legal or otherwise, and worse.

A morally strong society must be made up of self-disciplined people. Such discipline must be taught and ingrained from infancy. When this is done, virtuous people will be produced who will individually maintain a decent moral standard, regardless of peer opinion. Character is developed in the first few years of life. The training ground for our youth is the family. Even persons of high moral character don't have the patience to give to children other than their own, the first needed training, that which teaches children not to wet their pants, nor to run into the street without looking, that which teaches children not to have uncontrolled tantrums or take things from brothers and sisters. Outsiders cannot well present the needed lessons which parents teach their offspring out of love for them; lessons that are taught with instinctive understanding that they must be learned for the child's own good. The training that prepares a child to prosper in society cannot be well learned in other than a loving family (adopted children are usually loved as natural offspring and treated the same).

The instinct to procreate is coupled with a natural love for our offspring, also with an instinct to train them. To teach a child self-discipline first requires the same self-discipline in the parents. Try regimentation without showing affection concurrently. You will come up against natural rebellion and you will fail miserably. Love is a necessary ingredient to the development of the human being. Grown men often put up a gruff front, isolating themselves, claiming to be too tough to need love. We sometimes find women, out of fear of being hurt, avoiding entanglements (often wisely). Children, however, cannot develop properly in other than a secure and loving environment. Those who grow up without love and the training that goes with it, become anti-socials. They become criminals, the enemies of the law abiding society. We should feel great compassion for them. We should not, however, allow them to harm the society because their parents failed them. Two wrongs do not make a right. In fact, as a society, we must find the courage to protect our law-abiding citizens. If not, they will finally cease to be such. The results will be devastating.

The only environment that can create a moral society is the natural, normal and moral family.   We are at a point in time wherein many families are incomplete. Single-parent families can function and, in rare cases, do produce good rusults. The single parent bears a great burden. That parent must be esteemed when good results are achieved. It is easier and with a greater chance of success, however, when men and women can unite in love and harmony. Success is more probable when loving parents raise children to be productive, beneficial members of society; teach them to honor their parents and therefore honor **just Law**; teach them to be law abiding citizens who'll teach their own children to be the same.

Self-discipline is the key to morality.   Normal, natural families who understand natural principles are the key to a self-disciplined society. The many who belittle the family and propagate ideals of loose behavior for unmarried persons are peddling death and destruction. They are promoting it for themselves and those who choose to succumb to these wily, perverted priests of Baal. They are leading us to our demise as a nation. Mark you well! Without strong moral family government, our government will fall and become only a memory.

end of Essay 3

Essay 4

Self-discipline in large part means self-denial. The diabetic must control his or her diet and must exercise. Failure to do these things can result in blindness, failure of various organs and finally, in early death. Heart disease requires careful dieting and exercise. Most physical problems require careful self-regimentation, a lack of which has very measurable, negative results. The ability to control one's actions takes as much or more self-regimentation as must be exerted for physical well-being. The actions most difficult to control are those tied to emotions. Of course, like dietary regimen and physical exercise, self-control becomes easier through practice. The least obvious of human traits of course is our beingness, or our emotional and moral character.

To our society, the most important of the traits of its individual parts are their character, or their moral strength. Great self-disciplinary strength is necessary to military success. These strengths also reflect the stability and well-being of our society. Character weakness or immorality in civilians may not be as notable or as quickly damaging as in soldiers in the military. They, nonetheless, have insidious, long range effects on any society. They creep in and spread like cancer until entire societies crumble. We cut out cancer. We must cut out immorality if we are to survive.

The human being, like other animals, has a strong instinct to procreate. Without this, logic tells us we would not long be a part of this universe. Procreation requires the unity of both male and female. The normal among us are endowed with sexual drives, together with wonderful feelings for certain persons of the opposite gender. We are drawn together for natural relationships which perpetuate our race. Sexual activity is a natural, healthy, clean function which is attributed to morality when practiced properly. This activity must be practiced with control and under proper conditions.

Because sexual activity produces very serious results, it must be very carefully regulated. This regulation can only be accomplished by individuals who have developed morality through self-discipline. Results of illicit sexual activities are unwanted pregnancy, disease, emotional trauma and all the other problems that these things bring. The young can't have developed the ability to take responsibility for any of these problems. This means that parents or society are required to shoulder the responsibility of the results of youthful sexual activity. Even adults in many cases prove unable to be responsible for the results of imprudent relationships. In this area our nation has become permissive to a degree of stupidity or insanity.

We often find people made into role models for our youth, displaying themselves publicly in a manner not unlike some of the baser animals. We should probably not be offended when dogs copulate in public. People though, should not be allowed to do so, most especially on shows wherein great effort has been made to attract vast numbers of viewers of all ages.

Consider the incongruity of the following described scenario. Extensive advertising was done and large sums of money spent to create popularity, affection and respect for Elizabeth Taylor. She is very prominent in our entertainment world. She often appears publicly, demanding forcibly that our government increase spending on the AIDS problem. This means spending more of our (the people's) resources. She demands this spending to care for people ridden with the disease which she helps to propagate. This disease is promoted by presenting the idea that improper activity or attitudes are normal and even good. It is promoted by publicly advocating loose sexual behavior which is damaging to the health. Loose sexual behavior is contrary to the natural law of survival. Shame on anyone who promotes the loose sexual behavior which contributes to the spread of this disease. Shame on anyone who suggests that the bill should be increased upon the innocent.

Publicly advocating loose or unregulated sexual activity has helped create a tremendous economic and emotional burden on our society. It has helped create an environment wherein it is very difficult for morality to flourish. Any parent trying to teach children that sex is for responsible, married adults does so in the face of great opposition.

The television shows we all watch are designed by the most talented people money can buy. The shows are designed to convert our youth to their way of thinking. Television displays open, unregulated sex as attractive and as normal, proper behavior. It then joins in, authoritatively, with the conspiracy of government agencies and public schools to finish the job. They tell our youth that as they have no decent moral standard nor the intelligence to act responsibly, that they must coolly calculate and plan their immoral actions. Offered for inclusion in the plans are chemicals and mechanisms which have been proven to fail certain portions of the time. In other words, they tell our children that rather than abstain with one hundred percent security, they should participate and partially protect themselves. The protection promoted by these corrupt agencies and individuals, is for some of the time. Only one out of three or four times (the proven failure rate) will our children subject themselves to life shattering problems and possible death. Moths will fly into the flame and destroy themselves. We humans seem to feel a need to convert as many as possible to accompany us into the fire.

11

Thank the laws of nature that the conduct we've subscribed to as a society will result in **some** awakening in time. The law of opposites in all things will demand that some strengthen themselves and maintain honor. Some will even find the courage to attempt to show to our society the alternatives to self-degradation and destruction. Choose today to be among those who accept and teach that sexual relationships are only for the marriage bed. This will accomplish unmeasurable good in our world. Of course, many will sneer, so what! Let a few men and women separate themselves from the commonly accepted ideology of today. Let a few dedicate themselves to the idea that we can control ourselves and be moral. If this happens, the few can grow to many. As many as will develop moral strength will have a good chance at survival. Make your choice.

End of Essay 4

Essay 5

We all have a tendency to justify ourselves, or at least minimize in our minds, the seriousness of our negative actions. This is a mechanism, natural and necessary to our well-being. Part of the human make-up is our conscience. We instinctively shrink back from acts which will damage ourselves or others. Concurrently with twinges of conscience we tend to one degree or another to forgive ourselves or others. The trick, of course, is to strike a healthy balance. If we had not the ability to forgive, it would be as sorry a world as if conscience was absent. For our own, and our society's good, we must learn to forgive ourselves and others, only after we or they have ceased committing whatever unhealthy act and have made recompense, if appropriate.

There is no benefit to the society in forgiving a thief while he continues to steal from us. He must first recognize his own error and cease to do the damage. He must be sorry enough that he is willing to repair the damage and thereafter forever abstain. This is the healthy balance between conscience and the ability to forgive or show mercy. If we could not forgive, the incentive for the thief to change would be greatly diminished. The cost to us in suffering continued theft, or incarcerating or otherwise controlling him would be an ongoing burden.

The seriousness of a crime or offense against ourselves or society is measured by results or the harm done. Many damaging actions don't have immediately visible results and are not therefore declared illegal. Some of the most harmful actions, though, are those which cause whole societies to fall into harmful patterns of thinking and acting. Hitler, for instance, taught atrocious doctrines, preparing his people to perform the atrocities he espoused. In our country, many are pushing the liberalization of our moral standard. The result is acceptance and teaching in the guise of freedom, that anything goes. This misconstruing of the meaning of freedom is doing such damage as to make Hitler an insignificant piker by comparison.

On national television, on the Ron Reagan Show, supposedly renowned psychiatrists presented a diabolical theory. They claimed it is wrong to teach youth not to masturbate, wrong to tell youth it is harmful and should not be practiced. Don't be fooled by such idiotic nonsense. This is a lack of self-discipline and an act of self-gratification with no positive result. The failure of the individual to exercise self-discipline destroys that individual's ability to do so. We all have sexual appetites. We must have a dividing line of good or bad regarding the exercise of these appetites. The line must be drawn between negative and positive results.

13

The young boy who plays with himself hides to do so and feels shame. This comes from his conscience or nature's protective mechanism. Youth must be taught that self-regimentation is important. If youth is taught the opposite, "if it feels good, do it", the desires can soon overcome the objection or lack of it. The youth will learn to **not** control his urges. Once this lesson has been learned (lack of control), youth is totally susceptible to the great variety of tantalizing possibilities offered. We must teach our youth that the popular concepts of self-gratification do no good and are wrong. They must recognize their error, cease to commit harmful acts, forgive themselves and become strong productive members of the human family.

Today, our youth have been indoctrinated with the idea that anything is alright. Most sneer at the very idea that sex is only proper in marriage. The individuals, male or female, who come to marriage as virgins are a small portion among us. It is not necessary here to outline the terrible problems our nation faces, problems due to these loose or liberal attitudes toward our sacred ability for reproduction. Heterosexual promiscuity is a level of degradation which carries self-destructive results. Homosexuality and bestiality are yet a lower level in the advancement toward total abandonment of any control of self. Sexual deviations (from normal) are clearly the opposite of morality.

Homosexuals lurk everywhere to entice the youth who has already weakened his ability to regiment himself. Homosexuals who have abandoned all sense of honor and decency, offer all manner of enticements to our youth. When one takes that step into homosexuality, that person has finally told himself that his sexual desires are the prime-motivator in his or her life. That person has accepted the fact that sexual desires have complete control over him or her. This type of person can certainly not be considered as anything but a cancer on a strong moral society. A cancer which will surely consume unto death any nation which continues to tolerate it.

We now have so many homosexuals among us that they actually have political clout. We have supposed leaders who are either homosexuals themselves or are so greedy for power that they'll espouse any cause to gain desired positions. The religious "right" oppose them and cite biblical scripture to back themselves. The homosexuals, in turn, claim interpretive error of scripture and even join together in what they call religious organizations. How absurd!

Biblical law under any and all interpretation condemns unto death the practice of homosexuality and beastiality. There is no possibility for misunderstanding. These writings are clear and explicit. This can be looked at from a religious point of view. We simply take the position that nature demands that we protect ourselves to survive. There is no defense for homosexuality. If we allow it to flourish, we condemn ourselves to ultimate destruction.

This essay is a condemnation of homosexual activities. It is also an attempt to present the notion that we all can be far more than slaves to sexual gratification. We must control our urges rather than being controlled by them. Those among us who train ourselves to slavery will be unable to rise above it. We must begin to regiment ourselves and develop the strength of will necessary to enable us to ignore peer pressures. We must act responsibly ourselves and demand the same from our families and associates. We must draw the line between healthy, productive activity and that which will destroy us; self-gratification with no productive result. Choose this day whether you will be degenerate or decent. If decent, you must join the effort to propagate the same.

End of Essay 5

Essay 6

"Give me just ten who are stout-hearted men and I'll soon give you ten thousand more." These inspiring words are true. Strong individuals, when willing to do so, can gather more of the same together. Honor will seek honor. A cause is needed to stimulate the strong into actively seeking each other's company. The cause presented here is the survival of our nation. No argument is expected about the fact that evil begets evil and that our nation is in the throes of decadence. Evil begets evil and good begets good. Corruption though, seems to spread faster and more completely than does decency.

It seems that our guilt feels a need for company. Our conscience seems to allow us more latitude or easier justification if accompanied by other wrong doers. The idea seems to be that if every one does it, it must be alright. The truth is that if everyone does it we'd better take a hard analytical look. That which is popular today is more often than not detrimental. It is sometimes even life threatening to us as a people. The man to emulate is he who will maintain his integrity, even if the whole world reviles him for it. He who, if necessary, will stand totally alone in maintaining his principles.

Mothers of today, in large part, lack the natural affection for their children. This phenomena is too complex to have a simple root cause. Some of the more obvious reasons are greed for wealth, or for a less complicated life, or elevated positions among peers and a life of ease. The greed, in fact, has caused great selfishness. It causes men to abandon their children, looking out first for their own comfort, while forgetting the helplessness of their young. Mothers, greedy for the same things as are men, find the raising of children to be a heavy burden. Caring for the young inhibits their ability to have the comforts they've come to hold so dear. Many of our nation's mothers don't want to be such. Many want no children, or very few. The desire for self-gratifying sexual activity has not diminished with the loss of desire to propagate.

Great intellects have worked unceasingly in developing mechanisms and chemicals to help our society to avoid reproduction. Yes! It is now possible to gratify our reproductive urges with supposed impunity. We can gratify them with the expectation that we can avoid complications and responsibility for our actions. Many of the chemicals used have caused health problems. Of course our sophisticated medical scientists continue the quest, improving and making safer the methods. Medical science has succumbed to the will of the masses. They're helping us to become a people who can be taken over or controlled by our urges and be controlled by our desires for self-gratification. They are helping us to eliminate any need to regiment ourselves.

Reproductive control can be effectively practiced without demeaning ourselves. We can exercise restraint. We can abstain at times when fertilization is likely. We can exercise self-discipline which will of course, strengthen our ability for self-regimentation rather than destroying our ability by consciously planning lack of restraint.

We will not promote any particular church or sect. It seems appropriate though, to acknowledge the Catholics. They have, at least in the area of sexual morality, maintained the concept of the dignity of man. They've remained firmly opposed to abortions (infant murder) and to unnatural means of birth control. Among her ranks, this church has great opposition to these life saving, strength building regulations. Hail to the hierarchy of the catholics for their steadfastness in this area.

The controversy over whether it's in man's best interest to propagate his species is herein avoided. It is here stated emphatically that only one form of birth control is morally correct. The only form which fits within the realm of morality is self-controlled abstinence. Other forms, together with the planning of actions, with avoidance of responsibility, tear down and destroy man's dignity. They destroy man's ability to control his destiny and they create a decadent society.

Consider the men who had the courage and stamina, the self-discipline to winter in Valley Forge. Think how we must look to them. They suffered deprivation, cold, hunger and loneliness, away from their families. They were men determined to weather the storm, determined to fight for and achieve **LIBERTY**, for themselves and their posterity. They didn't give in to their every desire. They were stalwart, honorable men, the like of whom we seldom see.

You who have ears to hear and eyes to see, know that our progenitors gave their all. You know they gave even their life's blood to found our nation. They would be astoundingly repulsed to see our treatment of the heritage they left us at such a price. What anguish their hearts would suffer, seeing the terrible perversion of the wonderful Constitution they gave us, seeing it twisted to protect elements of corruption which destroy any and all who subscribe to them. Our progenitors would be sickened to see our Constitution so perverted that it demands that we suffer sodomy and advancement of the same as a cause, a Constitution so distorted that it allows human sacrifice or the mass murder of our unborn children.

Contemplate the program upon which our nation is about to embark. Men and women in the military, helping to defend our nation, are about to receive new requirements. They will have to work side by side with people who have sickening desires to violate them, people who have abandoned self-regimentation and cannot, therefore, be well-disciplined. Yes, our debased Constitution now, rather than defend the innocent, requires that they subject themselves to atrocities. Some call it freedom. You who have eyes to see and ears to hear, know that our forefathers would be sickened. Many of them would probably be unwilling to pay so high a price had they known how we'd tear down and tread asunder the wonderful freedom they left us.

It would be utterly impossible today for anyone with high moral principles to achieve an elevated political office. Votes come from pandering to a wide variety of greedy self-serving individuals or groups—pandering to groups, the agenda of whom is selfish, mostly corrupt and very damaging to our society. To achieve high office today, one must sell his soul to the Devil. One must agree to further the aims of the vast array of ideology spinners. These aims are greed, filth, oppression and even mass-murder. Yes, our elected leaders today are, per their own declarations of agreement, leaders of an evil Empire. We are an Empire that can no longer lead the world with idealistic principles. The wonderful democracy we've so actively pushed upon the world has become a show-place for every foul and evil thing that creeps or crawls upon the earth. In our zeal to expand our freedoms, we've forgotten to protect ourselves. We've allowed both government and individuals to trample our natural rights. All manner of annihilating practices occur every minute of every day throughout our land, practices which are eroding further any semblance of Liberty and Justice left among us.

We allow and even hail whore-mongery, homosexuality and beastiality. We commit widespread murder of the most innocent of all humans; our own unborn children. Decent humans must be appalled at the actions of today's society. The very horridness of this height of evil we've reached is causing a separation among us. This will continue until the strong have left the rest to their **just** desserts. The desserts will be weeping and wailing as they hack and slash themselves to pieces. It will take great strength and courage to stay out of the fray. Hunger will be prevalent. Only the very strong will avoid stealing or killing to feed their own. Criminal immorality will be rampant. Only the very honorable will abstain.

Pay attention, you who have ears to hear and eyes to see. You can no longer blot from your senses the degradation of our once so lovely nation. Anyone with a semblance of intelligence knows we became one of the greatest nations within recorded history. Intelligent beings know also that our greatness is fast fading. Those who established, fought for and built our greatness, were a special breed, special and far different from those who are now trampling it under foot— trampling the principles that raised us to such heights. Oh you perverters of all that is good. You who will desecrate the innocence of our lovely children. You who murder babies, or assure that they can have no clean habitation, no place in which to grow up into stalwart, healthy, productive people. We weep for the suffering you are bringing down upon your own heads. We anticipate joyfully though, the day that you will have eliminated yourselves from existence. The day when only the clean and the strong will be left, the clean and the strong who will re-establish <u>Liberty and Justice for all</u>.

You must choose which road to follow, choose to cease to commit acts which deteriorate your own strength and that of your nation. Forgive yourself what you must, having resolved to become morally strong and proud of it. We all do err. We all can overcome our weaknesses if willing. Choose to develop self-discipline and regulate our lives in a manner which will create persons of high integrity. Let us see if our Constitution might be saved in the spirit in which it was born. Let's see if we can turn the clock back a little. We must strengthen ourselves to resist the pervertors of our beautiful heritage.

"Give me some men who are stout-hearted men, who will fight for the right they adore. Give me just ten, who are stout-hearted men and I'll soon give you ten thousand more. Then, shoulder to shoulder and bolder and bolder they'll grow as they go to the fore. Then, there's nothing in the world, can halt or mar a plan, when stout-hearted men, can stick together, man to man."

The author of this song had great wisdom. He is joined in the supplication. Choose to be strong, healthy, wise men and women. Choose to raise up a generation of children giving them a chance for Liberty and Justice. Seek others with these desires and join with them.

End of Essay 6

Essay 7

Our propensity to be deceived is enhanced by our very human gravitation toward peer acceptance. The good opinion of those around us is indeed valuable to most people. Many of us fall into agreement with ideas or concepts just to get along. Some do so specifically attempting ingratiation with associates. This desire for social inclusion is very detrimental. It contributes greatly to the fact that the masses are easily led and as easily deceived. Crowds are often incited to riot. They are readily stimulated to join in self destructive practices or, evil. Hitler's success is just one recent, very clear example. Sadam Hussein is another. Many examples could be cited.

Our world records a history of the rise and fall of civilizations. Each and every great empire has, when at the height of success and prosperity, weakened morally. Degeneracy has spread like a virus through every affluent society. When the masses in any society have become ripe with corruption, the result has always been the fall. In our day, we have watched empires rise to great power, only to crumble. You who have eyes to see must know that popularity of ideologies or concepts do not make them right. In truth, most popular concepts should be suspect. Most people want to be decent, good and honorable. Most at the same time, however, feel a need to blend, or to be an integral part of the whole. This need is one of our baser qualities, it is akin to cowardice. The men and women needed to repair our nation must conquer this weakness. They must place personal integrity above peer acceptance or popularity. They must be willing to stand by their principles if it means standing alone. This kind of people, united in a good cause, will not fail.

Now come hard, cold facts. Truths that, though unpleasant, must be proclaimed in a loud voice to the world, but more specifically to this nation. The USA is the strongest nation on earth and mentor to leaders of nations the world over. We have infiltrated governments of all the nations of the earth, manipulating them toward our concepts. We've spent excessively in monies, weaponry and other favors, mixing in the affairs of all sovereign nations. We have purchased alliances or friends wherever possible, often aiding the side of our choice in national or internal disputes.

We have long since forgotten the good advice once hailed and accepted as our doctrine, i.e.,"Fair and equitable trade with all nations and entangling alliances with none." Our leaders, being heady with power, have entangled us tightly into the affairs of all the world. Though many hate us, they will sorrow greatly when we fall. We mix in the affairs of the world. We purchase their wares. We entice them to engage in trade with us, attempting to make them dependent upon us. This is a better way to control them than through force and with weaponry, though this option is sometimes used also. Control often gets beyond our ability.

Wisdom should have told our leaders long ago that the world is too big to be tightly manipulated by a few mortals. The fact that men manage to dupe the people into placing them into high positions over us does not make gods of them. It is seldom, though, that they can see this. Give power to a man and he quickly decides it is his *Just* due. He soon decides that he can do no wrong because his elevated position must mean that he is great and nearly infallible.

Having power in our government tends to give a sense of power over world affairs. It also gives a sense of the "rightness" of that power. Our leaders act like the "payer" of the prostitute. She is paid for favors, but when they tire of her, she is left to her own devices and is shunned. She can have no security beyond payment for the moment's performance. Most prostitutes begin to believe it can last. They are always abandoned. Any who hope for more will suffer dashed hopes. Neither can the nations of the earth expect long range security from us. Our leaders in their greatness are fickle indeed.

We often make small nations dependent upon us before pulling the plug. The little African nation of Somalia is one of the many with whom we have committed our whoredoms. We made her dependent upon us, then we abandoned her. Oh, how she has suffered. Now we are back doing it all over again. On the surface it seems a good idea to help her again. It may even be a legitimate obligation. We should not have meddled in the first place however, nor can we ever cure her ills.

It has never been legitimate for us to intrude in the affairs of other sovereign nations. No one has ever been helped long range, or in the end, by being allowed to become dependent upon another. Independence and self-sufficiency are necessary ingredients to self-esteem, which is necessary to well-being. Independence and self-sufficiency are the opposites of what we teach, by our actions, all over the world.

Aside from the wrongness of our fornicating with other sovereigns, we damage our own nation immeasurably. We are not spending our own money but that of future generations. Our children have not had the chance to vote on whether they will accept this slavery. They will be terribly oppressed if our society lasts long enough for them to be forced to pay for these foolishly wicked expenditures.

21

We tend to elect leaders already experienced politically, successful economically, and of course, well educated. "En mass", we praise and do homage to them. The high office holder, quickly develops great pride, which is the opposite of humility. The pride which gives the false sense of infallibility precludes prudence. Prudence of course, is the greater part of wisdom. It is a shame on man that his nature is such that power causes a diminishing of prudence and wisdom. To make matters worse, the longer one remains in power, the stronger grows the pride. This results in even further lessening of wisdom.

In this nation, "we the people" do choose our leaders. To a large degree therefore, we are responsible when prideful, evil men or women lead us. Many of us are too lazy to vote. Many others vote according to their perception of one's popularity. A large number of votes come from special interest groups who vote strictly for promotion of their own agenda. These groups seem to care nothing about fairness or the good of our nation. The complacent, leave selection of our leaders to those described above. "When the wicked rule, the people mourn." This is where we are and most of us, deservedly.

We have placed at our helm men and women of pride, who lack the wisdom to lead us with humility and honor. Our leaders truly believe it is their right to interfere in the affairs of the whole world and their actions prove that they believe it is our "right" to control the nations of the earth. This is why our government pays for favors from the leaders of nations of all the earth.

We elect our leaders. They then take our resources from us and use them to adulterate us with the peoples of the entire planet. We must accept the blame. We have allowed our government to become a massive, uncontrollable beast. One that has consumed our resources and those of our children for generations to come. They've consumed our wealth to spend it on themselves and on the world. One might see a certain justice in the current suffering of our people. We have done it to ourselves. Those who are to come, however, had nothing to do with creating this awful condition. Our forefathers suffered and died to give us freedom. We have given it up. Our children are sold into servitude. One can only speculate on how deeply enslaved we will become before the American producer quits.

The "gross national product" is considered to be the measure of our wealth. A true picture of our economic well-being must be calculated after deducting expenses from the income the products bring. Expenses in this context mean the cost of producing the goods plus the cost of government, bankers, insurances and legal services. Medical costs are not included because these costs are paid by the people (producers). Any medical expenses paid for by the government or insurance companies are paid for first by the people in taxes or insurance premiums. This is insane, because insurance premiums cost many times the amount of medical bills they pay. Government participation also costs far more than it should.

The "long and short" of our situation is plain. Producers in our country must yield sufficient goods to sustain themselves, the government, the bankers, insurance magnates and the legal system. Remember that government costs include the partial sustenance of the entire world. It does not take an economist to read our economic position. A newspaper delivery boy knows he must return to the publisher the value for papers delivered. If he fails to collect for some papers, he pays from his own funds. No one with even a minimum of elementary math skills can be so naive as to see anything but chaotic failure for our economy.

Accurate figures, establishing the quantity of producers against the number of people supported by them, probably cannot be acquired-neither can the value of our produced goods, as against the cost, be determined with precision. Hypothetical relationships are deduced, very conservatively, at approximately one producer per fifteen people who live off that one person's production. It is probably worse. The dollar cost is similarly estimated at many times the value of the manufactured goods in our "land of opportunity." Why do you think we have a government spending deficit? The average tax-payer is also the average consumer.

Let's analyze his purchase of a loaf of bread. The broker who bought the grain paid enough, so that the farmer could have a survival income after paying his costs—costs being direct production expenditures, plus interest on loans, insurances, legal fees and taxes. If the farmer's taxes are raised, what must he do to get the extra income needed? He must raise his prices. Who pays for the increase? Bear in mind that the broker has a certain "mark-up percentage," below which he will not drop. His "mark-up" includes enough so that he can retain some for himself after paying taxes, etc. Unless separate warehousing is involved, the miller comes after the broker. There are usually transportation companies along the way before the baker finally gets his materials. The miller and the baker get to purchase fuel and packaging materials from companies who have been through the same multi-tier cost gyrations. Ultimately the retailer gets his hands on the bread. He sets his prices to mark up the taxes etc., of all those who have gone before him. If taxes or any other costs are increased the retailer automatically raises the price to the consumer.

You can be certain that if taxes are raised on the wealthy, the increase is passed on to the consumer, with interest. The following information may need to be repeated several times. You will never understand national economics without an ingrained knowledge of the fact that the consumer pays for "everything." Never forget that all taxes, insurances, interest and legal services are paid for by the consumers of goods and services. Don't be beguiled into thinking that someone else will receive the tax increases, leaving you free from them. If there is a tax increase on anyone, you will help pay it. The wealthy, of course, pay taxes too. They are, however, in a position to pass most of their expenses on to the consumer. This means the masses of the people. The masses of the people (the consumers) are those who we call the middle and lower income classes.

"We, the people," have given our freedom over to greedy, power-mongers. We prefer to spend our time in self-gratifying frivolity. We refuse to be actively engaged in controlling "our government." We are now the blind being led by the blind. We can never again compete in world markets. Besides the terrible tax inequities, we pay vast portions of our resources to insurance companies. These leeches can only exist, because in our cowardice, we look for someone else to provide us with security. Insurance companies advertise the wonderful payouts they make in a few cases, so that millions of us will think insurance is a good gamble. How can anyone be so stupid as to believe you can get back as much as you put in? Most policies pay seventy five percent of the first years premiums to the agent. Beyond this the companies pay wonderful salaries to personnel. They provide buildings for their people to work in. How do you think they can do these things, make large profits and pay you back more than a pittance? They cannot!

The insurance companies have spent millions or billions paying our elected law makers to require that we contribute to them. Yes, by corrupt law, we must buy certain insurances. You can be sure of one thing with insurance companies. You can be certain that a minute portion of monies paid in will be returned to the payor. These companies exist for one purpose only—to change money from your bank to theirs. Do you know why hospital costs have risen so sharply? In large part, it is because insurance companies have bought a great many hospitals. They have driven the costs up so high that we know we can't pay without that wonderful insurance. No matter what the cost, insurance companies cannot possibly, ever, give a fair return to us, the fools who contribute to their vast fortunes.

Insurance has become a very large "required" cost of doing business in these United States. Our society, in its "cowardice," seeks someone to protect and provide for it. We are paying many times the value of supposed security that we are not receiving. The insurance problem is discussed because it is a large contributing factor in our inability to compete with world markets and should be exposed as such. It is just one of the many expenses that must be deducted from the value of our "Gross National Product" in determining our "economic well-being."

To a terrible degree we put tax upon tax upon tax. Our governing moguls spend many times more money than they have. The great insurance scam takes its toll. Our legal system adds more load onto the backs of the producers.

The problems discussed in this essay will soon have earth-shattering results around the world. Because we can no longer compete, we will continue to lose "market share". As "market share" is lost, our government's resources will dwindle. They will, of course, raise taxes. The problem is that "you can't get blood out of a turnip." As "market share" drops, so will employment. You cannot get much tax out of the unemployed. The time is not far off when creditors will no longer give us the rope with which to hang ourselves. Deficit spending will no longer be possible.

For all their supposed greatness, our godly leaders will have no more ability to commit their whoredoms with the governments of all the world. Imagine how many "Somalias" will surface around the world. The leaders of all nations will be devastated to lose us, the purchasers of their "good will". The world's production will no longer be bought by us. All the Economies of the planet earth will be in ruins. Our economy, which is interwoven with that of the world, will be among the first to collapse. We will have no government. Anarchy will reign supreme in this country. We will have no immigration problems. No one will dare set foot on our soil. They will stay back, watching and weeping, at least till the murdering, looting and the burning subside. These will subside only when the majority of our population no longer lives.

Take heart! A brighter day will come. Some courageous, honorable men and women will pull out of the mess. They will gather together to rebuild our world. **Liberty**, will once again be established.

The conditions herein discussed are the results of greed and pride. These are in perfect harmony with the total lack of morality to which our nation now subscribes, the immorality which is the subject of this series of essays, and the immorality that is causing the "**down-fall**" of our once, so lovely nation.

There is but one possible salvation for any of us. We must rally around a standard of morality which will require respect for each others **rights** and also the "rights" of other sovereign nations. We will either do this as a nation or fall. We can take heart from the knowledge that **some** will rally. **Some** will pull away from the chaos and make preparations to rebuild.

End of Essay 7

Essay 8

This is a further effort to sketch the present "human condition". Primary discussion in this essay will pertain to our excessive greed and the results to society's well-being. Back-up documentation is intentionally ignored in this work. The author accepts the premise that most of his peers have reasoning power. It is hoped that the reader will consider these contents carefully and will meditate regarding the validity of doctrine set forth herein. Most of us, if desirous of truth, can deduce it. One key is to be truly prepared to accept "what is", whether it agrees with our desires or not. The author hammers at this theme over and over.

You, dear reader, must understand that if you want truth, you must be willing to ignore popular opinion. You can discern for yourself or join the crowd and be duped. While we have powers of discernment, we will fool ourselves if we preconceive the truth or expect it to fit or serve our own interests. These are basic principles which are repeated throughout these essays. Without this understanding, this work will certainly not edify you, even a little.

In these writings, terms such as good, bad, righteous, evil, diabolical, right or wrong, are adjectives describing actions relating to our society. If an action is evil, it is so because of damage done to people thereby. Good things are healthy for any or all of us. Bad things are harmful. Among the most evil of man's baser traits is greed. It is synonymous with jealousy, covetousness and selfishness. It is the cause of many infractions against man's inalienable rights.

The earth, together with nature, provides us with all human needs. We are born with the ability to subdue the earth and glean from it, comforts far beyond requirements for health and happiness. Consider this truth: Every man, woman and child on this globe could be wealthy by today's standards. This could only result though, through a system of perfect equity. Equity for all can't exist in the face of mass greed.

Mother earth provides resources. Energies from celestial bodies unite with our terrestrial potencies to create wonderful power sources. We have but to harness and direct these elements. Yes, we could have almost free energy. A few governments have dabbled with solar, wind and hydraulic systems and have proven the possibilities. Little benefit has been realized though for mankind. When governments find income sources, they also find ways to spend (waste) them.

Organic farming methods, together with crop rotation and the principle of periodically resting the land, preserves the soil and produces much healthier crops. Quicker, higher yields can be achieved though, with chemical fertilizers. The chemicals are used by most farmers in our country. The result is vast areas of "burned out" land which no longer produces enough to be profitable. Nature has wonderful recycling abilities. Man has the capacity to both separate and compile compounds in such a way that recycling becomes difficult and slow for natural processes. Greed has led us to do this excessively.

If man's greed would allow him to continue, elemental nature would eventually be unable to keep ahead of us. Given enough time and technology, we certainly could "lay waste" sufficiently to inhibit earth's ability to sustain large populations. Alas! we cannot control ourselves well enough to survive (en-masse) long enough for the greedy to destroy our habitat. Our selfishness causes so such contention among us that even our ability for evil is limited. We will destroy ourselves before we do the planet.

> A group of great intellects can perform wonders.
> Disharmony reigns and mostly brings blunders.
> Mob rule of the wicked will end in a flood.
> They will rend from themselves a river of blood.
> The few who are decent and honest and true,
> Will rebuild our nation, with Justice anew.

Greed can be subtle and confused with healthy ambition. They needn't be synonymous, but very often are. Security, health and comforts are legitimate human desires. Craving these to the exclusion of all else usually turns into covetousness. Avidity for more than our needs can easily turn into a greedy mania. When in this condition, men and women invariably exclude morality from their systems.

Greed travels beyond financial wants. Lust for the adoration of peers or craving power over others are typical characteristics of it. A propensity to satiate various forms of lust often accompanies the rapacious. This is the condition of the majority of our citizens.

Many point out the lunacy of our government and rightly so. The government is truly a reflection of ourselves in this democracy. It is formed by gluttonous self-interests for no other purpose than to further their own ends. The successful politician learns to succor the aspirations of a diversity of selfish factions. He must convince organizations that he will push their agenda. They, then, for their own gain, contribute to empowerment of their man. Honor, integrity, decency, and even the good of our nation are ignored. Most votes are cast on a basis of: "what will be done for me?"

We have today, large blocks of voters, recipients of pensions from government posts. The majority of these spent a much shorter time earning retirement than did most in the private sector. Pensions though, for government employees (including military) greatly exceed in both amount and longevity, those available to workers in the private sector. If you are pensioned from government service, here is a chance to test your ability to discern truth. Consider this: most people do not, as generally alluded, give their lives to the service. Most work or put in their time for the pay they receive and for no other reason. The pension, of course, is part of it. The reimbursement package is the motivator, not a philanthropic desire to serve. Very few people give their lives to government, military or other employment groups. Most sell their services for pay.

Where does the money come from to pay government salaries and pensions? We all know that it comes from production of goods and services, the private business world. Why do we citizens allow ourselves to be taxed so heavily (multi-tier), and to have our earnings dispersed so unfairly? Should those who generate our means (the producers) be forced to provide far greater comforts and security for those who do not produce than they themselves (the producers) can have? Is it fair to pay our supposed servants more than we can earn? Those of you on the receiving end will be hard put to admit the truth. Those who are suffering won't have much trouble with it.

The meek or the less aggressive among us are unquestionably the producers of our wealth. The more aggressively ambitious seek positions wherein they can more greatly benefit from the production of others. Yes! ambition can be healthy, especially when one is willing to improve circumstances through higher personal production. Ambition has turned to greed when one decides to improve one's position with a larger share of another's production. When earnings are taken from the producer and given to the non-producer, seeds of discontent are sown. The meek will tolerate such a condition. The greedy capitalize on this.

The greedy always gain power over the less aggressive. They cannot exercise restraint. They must take **more** and **more** and **more**. The producer, by nature, will accept inequities. Don't be fooled into believing though, that there is no limit to his or her patience. They are too well educated now and know instinctively that greedy power mongers are using them badly. They will be pushed too far. They will rebel.

We were given a marvelous form of government. Wonderfully wise and selfless men, many of history's greatest, wasted their lives and fortunes to provide us with **freedom**. They left us a form of government which should provide liberty and justice for all. Equity is synonymous with justice. You cannot have one without the other.

Greedy, lustful men have usurped power over us, changing our laws and trampling our Constitution under-foot. Only greed could accomplish this. Short of a terrible calamity, only selflessness could undo the damage.

Here is a key with which to judge actions of our law makers and our interpreters (the supreme court). **Laws passed or interpretations given, which mete out other than equitable justice, are contrary to the spirit of our Constitution**.

Using previously set precedence is the general rule in our Judiciary System. The framers of our Constitution were exceptionally wise men. They gave us the best that could be had. Precedence should therefore have kept us on the right track.

A bad precedence can be built upon as well as a good one. Active greed inhibits wisdom. Evil, greedy men can easily make ever so subtle changes in precedence, almost without detection. This has happened to the Constitution of the United States of America. Our Constitution now defends the greedy, the usurper, and the criminal against the innocent and the meek. A myriad of examples could be cited, but the reader would tire of so lengthy a document. Brief mention of a few circumstances will suffice for the honest in heart. Nature will ultimately give justice to all others.

Our Constitution gave us the right to quick and sure Justice. Do you think this was meant to protect the criminal? Logical truth tells us it was meant to protect the innocent from the criminal and also to protect the innocent against wrongful conviction. We have allowed lawyers (law makers) for their own greedy purposes to pollute and obliterate our right to quick, sure justice.

If you fall victim to theft or a member of your family is raped or murdered, you are usually penalized more than the criminal. You are taxed to provide for him and often for his family. You usually pay for his defense, generally exorbitantly. After the criminal is found guilty, you pay for stays, appeals and all manner of legal maneuvers. You pay his medical expenses, often better care than you can afford for yourself. You support him and others to care for him—all this because he damaged you and your society. This is the result of greedy law makers, having created for themselves, a lucrative niche at your expense. We pay very handsome salaries to Supreme Court Justices. We give them homage. They have not defended our Constitution. They have torn it to shreds. Oh, the shame, we have allowed it.

Does the fact that our government has adulterated itself gives us license? No! Our government comes from us. We have created this monster. What can be done to tame and correct our *servants*? We must conquer our own greed. We must be willing to selflessly proselyte our peers. We must accept the spirit of our Constitution, teach others and push all enlightened citizens to the polls. Rather than accept those who come seeking office, let's seek out some men of honor and convince them to serve.

If you can see and accept truth, you are sorely needed for an attempt to save our nation. If you will accept truth and teach it, our Constitution might be stitched back together. Remember the key: **If justice is not served, the intended spirit of our Constitution has not been followed**. Remember too, that justice is not served when the innocent pay for the acts of the criminal. Neither is justice served when that which you earn is taken and given to him who did not earn it.

Needed to save our nation or rebuild it are selfless, moral, courageous individuals, who can unite as did our progenitors. Certain characteristics, prevalent among us, must be analyzed. If you can base your analysis on truth, regardless of your state of being, you have a chance at survival and participation. If you cannot accept truth because acceptance will require unacceptable change, you cannot help.

Excessive greed has caused most people in our society to lose sight of that which has true value. We seek after monetary gain, fame and power. These are held up as paramount goals. Each of these in excess has little or no true value. None of these can bring happiness or tranquility. None of them can have impregnable duration. Monetary wealth must be guarded and constantly manipulated. Power and fame are even more fickle.

Because of greed, our society places value on all the wrong things. It is now unquestionably evident that our monetary system is doomed. The deficit that has supplied so much political mileage cannot be brought under control. The pensioners will tolerate no cut-back, nor will any of the strong recipients of "entitlements". The glorious "*people's representatives*" don't dare cut the take for their backers. The deficit will continue to grow. Yes, it will reach a point where the diminishing numbers of producers can no longer cover the payments.

Yes, the people will one day soon, "en masse", realize that our money is worth exactly the value of the paper. Being used paper, that value will be small indeed.

When money is unavailable for sustenance of the government, the power will also be gone. The lust for power will, in that day, come to naught. You great leaders will have no followers. Without the simple exchange medium, theaters, television networks and other entertainment centers will close. Those who thrive on adoration from the masses will find it no more. How painful it will be for so many to lose all that they've held dear.

Those among us with wealth, power or grandeur, will suffer terrible losses. The author weeps more though, for the masses. This society has "en masse", become so greedy as to put money, comforts and self ingratiation ahead of all else that our world offers. One would think that possessions would be valued by their "potential to give joy". Nay, not so! Nothing in life can bring the joy one has in one's children. This is an eternal truth which will be accepted by many. More though will reject it, as they have no experience from which to judge. So very many today have refused themselves the joy of children, seeking instead the perishing wealth of our dying world. Oh! what a miserable lot we are.

We have all watched heirs fight with family members over paltry inheritances. People cheat and steal from each other for possessions they had nothing to do with earning. Families are ripped apart for small estates they usually lose or quickly spend.

Great joy is found in him who can take pride in his integrity. Can anyone take pride in having underhandedly out-maneuvered his fellow man to get gain from him? Who can find tranquility while greedily seeking every advantage over everyone at every moment? You cannot let up without falling behind. If you stumble, others will trample you in their mad rush toward goals similar to your own.

The pressure created in this nation from the greed of our people has caused mass insanity. The pressure created by our greed is greater than we can bear. We cannot survive such madness. The mass murders, the sexual deviations, and the wholesale slaughter of our own innocent unborn children, are the result of the unbearable weight. Our greed has created stress which is beyond our ability to control. The pressures have created for us this calamitous condition from which there may be no salvation.

Take a long hard look. Do you really want to grow old with no one to love or be loved by? Do you really believe that pursuing fame or fortune is as valuable as producing live human offspring? Can wealth, power or fame truly be worth as much as development of knowledge and honor and deserved respect—most especially, respect from your own family?

If you grow old and are alone, you'll have little joy. If you have a child to love, you'll be more complete. Several children, can give you more joy than any other source. Learn another truth: children do not need the wonderful advantages usually planned and seldom realized; they are better off with a modest existence, wherein they have to contribute. The children who learn responsibility at an early age are those who will bring joy to their parents in the long run.

As a people, our only salvation will be a return to decency. We must put aside the greed which is the root cause of most of our immorality. Decide for yourself whether the following statement is true. "Continued greed-driven immorality, will surely destroy this people." As many as can overcome this evil can become worthy to associate with those who will rebuild our honorable society.

End of Essay 8

Essay 9

Liberty through law is the topic of this essay. Discussed will be the need for "just" law and the problems resulting from absence or corruption of the same.

Government has but one legitimate function—the protection of the governed through "just" administration of "just" laws. Page six of Frederic Bastiat's treaty, "The Law", states that "law is the collective organization of the individual right to lawful defense." Bastiat was right. The need for collective organization for lawful defense of individuals is the only justification for establishment of governments. Governments that do more or less than this are of no benefit to their citizenry.

History shows us a great diversity of ruling bodies. The majority of them have fallen far short of legitimate function. Most have, in fact, become oppressive to the people rather than defensive.

Human nature causes the more aggressive to usurp power over the placid among us. The power hungry invariably gain advantage and use it to reinforce their positions of eminence. Governments can only rule with the consent of the people. Withholding of consent though, can become very difficult. Usually, ruling bodies, subtly, gradually, surely, strengthen themselves to positions of firm entrenchment, while becoming overbearing. It is then difficult to dislodge them.

People have to be pushed far beyond acceptable limits before they will rebel. Horribly tyrannical governments often last long enough to perpetuate immense amounts of misery.

This treatise deals with the United States of America, our government and our laws. Though the synopsis could fit many societies, it is tailored specifically to ours.

The author feels a compulsion to warn his compatriots, or the citizens of this nation of impending doom and also to advise all who will listen that we could yet heal ourselves. If we try and fail, through the effort, many will develop the courage and strength to see themselves through the calamitous times ahead. Those who make the valiant effort are those who, if necessary, will rebuild, after many of us have looted, burned and killed most of our own.

Our government was initiated in order to **"form a more perfect union"**, a union that would guarantee to its citizens, the right to **"life, liberty and the pursuit of happiness"**. To this end, independence was declared and a great war was fought. After victory, at enormous cost, some of history's wisest men, established for us a wonderful constitution. This was done for one purpose only. It was to provide us with the guarantee, which the declaration says we have a right to. It was framed to give us **"Liberty Through Law"**.

Freedom for any society can be achieved only under "just" laws. Do you have enough intellect and maturity to recognize this truth? Freedom does not mean license to do as we choose to others. It means the opposite. A **law of liberty** protects man's **"inalienable rights"**. It sets forth our legitimate entitlements protection-wise. It creates both statutes and judgements. Statutes define actions which must or must not be committed. Judgements establish enforcement methods, including penalties for infractions against statutes. Corrupted law (such as ours), fails to enact statutes protective of the citizens. Ineffective law (such as ours), fails to execute fair judgements. Standing on your head for several hours a day will accomplish as much good as statutes without effective judgements.

Respect for law has greatly diminished in our country. This is natural in view of the fact that, for so long we have had so few, honorable administrators, thereof. Our system is now saturated with a myriad of stupid, unnecessary and many evil, enslaving statutes. Our educational system has been terribly neglectful in this area. Children are no longer taught principles of right and wrong as they pertain to responsibility to society. Emphasis is placed, rather, on teaching our children how to avoid natural penalties for illicit behavior. Our youth is taught or shown on every hand, tenets of vile wickedness. Will you read it if many examples are cited? Probably not, illustrations will therefore be brief.

An area that has, by corrupt legal statute, cost the American public billions of dollars is insurance. We have deviated a great deal from true capitalism. Great strides have been made into socialism. Our socialism has resulted in large part from the immorality of the people. This has allowed greed to become the norm. The greedy take all they can through duping or sales promotion methods. Their next logical step is to invest in corruption of politicians. This has resulted in "purchased law", which requires that we buy insurances at exorbitant prices. This, of course, adds to the cost of our goods and services. We pay more for everything. That we cannot compete in world markets is due mostly to our greed and to our corrupted laws.

Since automobile insurance became mandatory in the state of Texas, the cost has increased approximately five hundred percent. This is close to one hundred percent per year. Of course, we all enjoy the feeling of protection against damage from someone unable to respond. Our "purchased law" has simply made it far too expensive. The people were suffering already from excessive tax burdens and many other outrageously overpriced necessities. The venomous insurance industry has added greatly to our load. To require responsibility is legitimate. To establish the method, favoring the greedy is illegitimate.

In the 1930s, some idiotic politicians came up with a *brilliant* vote- getting idea. They proposed a plan to provide for us in our old age. This quickly turned from voluntary to mandatory for all who had incomes. One wonders how our world survived till that point in time. The social security (forced government insurance), evolved into a tax which far exceeds the payback. It was very profitable for the government. The large group of retirees though, became a united voting bloc. The whores on Capitol Hill gained yet another purchaser of their wares, one who packs a big stick vote-wise.

The retired Americans, as a united lobbying group, have coerced our !!!congress into including payment for medical costs, over and above retirement incomes. Medicare on the surface seemed legitimate and good. Remember the saying: "You can't make a silk purse out of a sow's ear?" Don't forget that when you take from the producer to give to the non-producer, you have started on the road to self-destruction. Don't forget either that you cannot discern truth unless you're willing to accept it even if it disagrees with your personal desires.

When our beloved government began the program of forced insurance, they sealed our doom, health-care-wise and prideful self-reliance-wise. The result is that most citizens in the USA are no longer psychologically secure in their own adroitness. We were once a nation of individuals, confident in our ability to provide for ourselves. The football team that can achieve euphoric self assurance can't be beaten. The team that loses confidence can be beaten by inferior opponents. We are now a society of snivelers who feel that though we can't do it for ourselves, the insurance companies or the government will provide. Now the social security taxes are not sufficient, so our glorious government is borrowing from our grandchildren. Who will they (our posterity), borrow from to pay for their forced insurances?

Fear not! some producers remain. Our glorious leaders will take from them to care for the rest. Each producer today has only to provide for fifteen or twenty drones. A few years from now it will be forty or fifty. Who can say how many will be supported by each fool before the dupes simply quit. One need not be a prophet to accurately prophesy the end-result to our present course.

The medical industry has a history of struggle and self-sacrifice. Very evidently, medical practitioners "**were**" honorable, dedicated people, who sought to alleviate suffering among their fellow men. The "Hippocratic Oath" was developed during the time that this was so. Today it sounds ridiculous, in view of the greedy, self-serving, murderous medical profession we are serving. Medical doctors became so honored that they were finally given power of choice over life or death. Doctors are as human as politicians. Most are corrupted by the honor given them and the opportunities that have developed for greed.

It is probable that a very small number of medical doctors could maintain some integrity. The milk of human kindness must be present in many of them as they begin. The unnatural glorification though, works to overcome their decent side. Add to the public adoration, the laws which give them illegitimate powers and the ability to charge exorbitantly. This wondrous group has about as much chance as do politicians, lawyers and preachers of maintaining humility and honor.

Wonderful opportunities are provided by Medicare, Medicaid, welfare systems and private insurance companies (many are owners of medical facilities). The medical profession has been unable to resist the temptation. They have become greedy, self-serving, gluttons. They routinely prescribe unnecessary tests, care and surgery, designed to transfer all their patients' resources to themselves. Our medical institution has turned from one of great honor, to one feared as a group of greedy, evil, murderous racketeers.

Our Constitution has been **corrupted**. Our laws are **perverted**. Instead of protecting the innocent, we now propagate practices which ignore the rights of the meek, or the weak. We take from this group everything, from the fruits of their labor to their very lives. The weaker and more innocent, the greater the danger.

Originally, our Constitution was very similar to that of ancient Israel. Theirs consisted of ten basic tenets, with a few ramifications and explanations. It was a very simple law which protected the innocent from the criminal. Early Christians called it the **Perfect Law of Liberty**. Biblical history shows a period of between twelve and thirteen hundred years wherein **God's** chosen people, the Israelites, prospered and suffered according to the degree that they kept their part of the covenant to keep **God's Law**, the ten commandments. They prospered, becoming a powerful and wealthy nation when they complied with the **Law**. Per their historians, when they relaxed their standards, changing their laws and failing to execute judgements, they became too weak and disorganized to defend themselves.

Our nation was formed by Christians who understood the wisdom of the Israelite law. In our Constitution, they provided us with the ability and the duty to establish similar statutes with fair judgements. Early in our life as a nation, the laws throughout the states paralleled very closely those of ancient Israel.

The modern Christians, like most modern Jews (at least in the USA), have **"religionized"** the Ten Commandments. These civil statutes and judgements which require that men respect each other's rights are set aside as law. They are now religious tenets to be aspired to by the pious, but are not requirements. When laws that keep men free are trampled or done away with, of course freedom is lost.

The Jews watered down their laws. The Christians (of today) accept this and blame it on their Christ. They claim he replaced the requirement to respect each other's rights with admonitions to love one another. Certainly, if people love one another, this will deter infringements. Societies have proven through all the ages though, that very small portions of the people will ever attain to this love. Even the Christians, who stress love, show it only for their own kind. Most of them accept their own and belittle or even curse all others.

The founders of our Constitution did not attempt to keep religion out of government. They did attempt to guard against individual sects gaining control. These men of wisdom understood how intolerant religious groups are toward each other.

As a nation, we have relaxed our standards. We have changed our law, ignoring the spirit of our Constitution. We have, to a great extent, failed to pass judgement. Our laws today, rather than defend our freedom, make us slaves to the whims of fools. They also subject us to the will of the greedy. The enforcement officers in our system are "canonized" by the magistrates. They are a law unto themselves.

Murderers, rapists, molesters, receive very mild sentences. They are then provided for by the society they have harmed. In many instances, the greater penalties are meted out for crimes that do very little harm. Many innocent actions are made into crimes through the purchase of law-makers. We all are criminals unless we conform to many unconstitutional statutes which add to the corruption of our nation.

The haughty, power-mongering politicians and law makers are not solely responsible. We, the people, have always had enough power through the vote to have maintained freedom. We've given up our liberty through lazy, lackadaisical abstention from our duty. By being unwilling to defend the innocent, we've come to deserve to suffer from the rampant criminality.

We still have the ability to correct our corruption. We can return to our Constitution in its purity. We can, with the power of our vote, regain freedom. It will take great dedication and willingness to proselyte (teach and extol) all with whom you can gain audience. This is the only possibility for the peaceful salvation of our nation. The alternative is horrible suffering during self destruction.

Preach liberty. Teach the true meaning of freedom. Our progenitors (nationwise) could not guarantee our inalienable rights for all time. They were able only to give us the ability to maintain them for ourselves. We have failed to do so, but we can regain them if we will. We deserve freedom, only if we're willing to guarantee it to our peers also. If we want it we must pay the price.

Because our freedoms have so greatly deteriorated, it will now take great effort to restore them. It will not happen without a sufficient number of highly dedicated people. This means moral people, because the immoral do not want "Liberty For All". It will curb their ability to infringe on the rights of others.

Morality, in a nutshell, means acceptance of responsibility for all our actions and the willingness to abstain from actions harmful to ourselves and others. If you extol your people toward morality, you are simply asking them to seek greater health and happiness. Is this not a worthy endeavor? Will you do it?

Are you willing to defend our nation by teaching and admonishing freedom through law? Are you willing to return to the spirit of our Constitution before it became polluted? Do you want liberty for yourself and your children? If so, then remember the following. Etch it into your memory so that you never lose sight of it:

Our Constitution provides for the passing of laws, only for the purpose of maintaining justice. Without justice, freedom cannot exist. When law is interpreted by legal precedence, if justice is not done, the precedence is bad or the interpretation faulty. If justice is not served by our legal system, it is not acting in the spirit of our Constitution. When a decision is evidently unfair but legal, the law is corrupted. When judges will base decisions on precedence while abstaining from fairness, they are not fit to be judges.

Just law must be simple. Justice is diminished when laws become complicated. Remember that protection of the innocent is the only

legitimate function of our legal system. Willingness to protect the innocent among us is what entitles us to our inalienable rights. We have no claim on this entitlement if we are unwilling to defend it for ourselves and our neighbors.

How can we defend the innocent? We must stop the criminal. Is this complicated? It has become so. Our laws have been made by lawyers. They have ignored our Constitution to complicate our laws. This is criminal. How could we have allowed it? We have because so many among us are criminal and hope to avoid justice. Many more are simply lethargic.

This essay can be summed up in just a few words. Our entire legal system, to be fair, must be guided by the same simplicity. This summation is the simple definition of the meaning of **"inalienable rights"** Our Constitution was established explicitly for the purpose of maintaining these rights. Greed and lethargy have caused us to abandon the maintenance of them.

Those who declared for us, independence and established our Constitution, did so based on the following belief; "Men are endowed by their Creator with certain **inalienable rights**."

Our **inalienable rights** are the right or freedom to do anything we choose with only one limit. Anything we choose except to infringe on the rights or freedoms of others. Is this difficult to understand? Not the least bit. Do whatever you like, so long as no one is harmed by your action.

Do homosexuals solicit or propagate their immorality? Do they spread a deadly disease through sodomy? Does this harm anyone?

Some people, for the sake of argument, claim we can't prove that unborn babies are real people. I tell you that they **damn sure can't prove otherwise**. We all know that unborn infants are as alive and as human as anyone. The only ones who will deny this are those who wish freedom to infringe on the rights of others.

Women should all have the right of choice, choice to abstain from participation in creating unwanted life. Once they've made their choice though, and have made a baby, they cannot act without affecting **its** rights. You only deserve protection of your freedom if you are willing to defend that of others. If you're willing to murder the most innocent of all among us, there can be only one **just** penalty.

All judgements should be imposed quickly and surely. The purpose of penalties is not vengeance. It is the defense of the innocent. When we execute murderers, the intent is not to harm them. It is done to prevent further atrocities by them. Yes, we could keep them penned-up forever. This penalizes the society that has to provide for them. It is not fair that we should work our lives out to care for those who harm us. If care of criminals was given on a volunteer basis, some justification might be found. It is not done this way. We are taxed. See what happens if you fail to pay your taxes.

Our penal system needs much reform. It could, and should be, self supporting. Be that as it may, our society by coddling criminals, fails to defend the innocent. This constitutes a criminal society. In forcing us to pay taxes to support criminals, our government is criminal.

The legislators and judges who have brought us to this state are traitors of the worse kind. They have enslaved a once wonderfully free people. As is pointed out earlier, we are guilty with them. We have tolerated and even sought after the resultant **destruction** of our Constitution and hence, our **liberty**.

It must be repeated. **Our Constitution never gave us license to infringe on the freedoms of our fellow men. Freedom was provided for all actions, excluding only that (harming others).**

Forsake greedy criminality. Dedicate yourself to honorable decency. Help to restore us to glorious liberty under law. Take part in reestablishing our Constitution, including statutes and judgements that protect the innocent.

End of Essay 9

Essay 10

All is rotten. All is dross and refuse. The stink of our decomposition rises to the heavens. Open your eyes my people. See the folly of your decadence. Un-stop your ears. Hear and fear for the end of your world is near.

> The world as we know it is fading.
> Evil abounds everywhere.
> Freedom and right go cascading,
> Into the depths of despair.
>
> Hysteria is rampant
> Everywhere round our sphere,
> The spirit of doom is dominant.
> Disaster is very near,
>
> Our nation has gone a whoring,
> Throughout this world of ours.
> So now must come the warning.
> It's written in the stars,
>
> That evil begets evil
> With wars and rumors of wars.
> Yes, its begun, the upheaval
> To destroy from our heights to our shores.
>
> The life blood of this people
> Will like water flow.
> Rotting flesh on every hand,
> Will healthy maggots grow.
>
> We' ve turned from the Law of Liberty
> The law that kept us free.
> So we must pay the penalty.
> We must fight and die or flee.
>
> In giving up our freedom,
> We've offered up our lives.
> By mingling with Sodom,
> We've dug our early graves.

The murder of our un-born,
The grinding of their flesh,
Assures that our leaders will be shorn
Of any hope that God might bless
Their efforts from now on.

This nation's god is money,
Or Mammon if you please.
And those who worship this false god
Will never more know peace.

For money is intangible.
It comes and then it goes.
And you who are more fanciful,
Whose money grows and grows
Will anguish more than all the rest
When into dust it flows.

Your god is doomed to failure.
Your mammon cannot stand.
So, soon you'll lose your savior
He'll vanish from the land.

Your banks will all go under.
What's the paper worth?
In piles and heaps it will be burned,
Throughout the planet Earth.

You will not parent children.
The cost is far too great.
You'd rather go a whoring,
Then kill the damned ingrate.

Yes kill the little bastard.
Who does he think he is,
To infringe on your planned standard?
Your life of wealth and ease.

So bow you down and deify
Your fancy clothes and cars,
Your jewelry, furs, your money.
Praise them to the stars.

And when they cease to be,
Your graven deity,
You'll weep and wail and try to flee,
But no one will deliver thee.

You've given up morality.
A life of ease you cherish.
You now must face reality.
Your decadence must perish.

Yes! "*All is rotten.*
All is dross and refuse."
Yes, oh woe begotten,
We've made our world thus.

There is a God in Heaven.
He gave this earth to us.
With very few requirements,
He says we must be Just.

He says his children must be free.
He gave the Law of Liberty.
He says he cannot tolerate,
Corrupt conditions we create.

Once again he'll cleanse the earth
Of those who prove they have no worth.
Those who trample truth and right.
And justice quell with all their might.

Those will remain who freedom love,
Who will forsake inequity,
And grant that Liberty from above
Is right for all who deserve to be.

Natural Law cannot be tampered with without consequences. *For every action there is an equal and opposite reaction. What goes up must come down. Barring outside influence, an object dropped from a height will fall in a straight line.*

Love begets love. Hatred begets hatred. Crime begets crime. Laughter stimulates laughter. Grief finds sympathetic grief. Truisms all. Yes, much about our existence is simply the way it is. Much cannot be changed by man or by any power that be. Take from a man that for which he has worked and struggled. Take it through theft in the night or by deviously gained, corrupted bureaucratic power. He hates the thief in the night. Neither can he love the "legal thief".

Of course, sudden theft carries some shock and seems more personal than theft by the powers that be. Government, or governing agencies have had a cloak of seeming legitimacy. Even now, many of us (maybe most) feel that the many government programs are justified.

Of course, governments can perform advantageous functions for society. While governments limit themselves to serving the people from whom they supposedly get their power, they can be of great value. They can even merit respect. As with with other entities, however, moderation in all things is the key to maintaining a logical and useful equilibrium. Excesses invariably cause imbalance in the lives of individuals, organizations and governments.

Moderation usually does little harm. Intemperance always does damage. A little wine is healthful. Large quantities can be devastating. Whether it be in drinking, eating, in actions or lack of them, in punishment or lack of it, there is a line which separates good from bad. Temperance is good. Excesses invariably are harmful.

Our society today must be described as intemperate. From the lowest to the highest among us, immorality is rampantly excessive. We have become truly, gluttonously decadent and our gluttonous government no longer serves us, the people.

Frederic Bastiat, over a hundred and fifty years ago, described the condition of his French Society. In many respects, that society was similar to ours today. It was riddled with corruption. It had become excessively socialistic. In socialism, as Bastiat points out, the fruits of the labor of the producer must be taken from him. This is the resource needed to support those who produce little or nothing.

When a government takes from its producers to give to its non producers, it sows the seeds of its own destruction. This is not because great statesmen and jurists like Bastiat, Blackstone and others, have declared it to be so. This is an irrefutable fact of nature which cannot be changed. A Truism.

All natural men have an irrepressible instinct to survive. Infringing on the ability to do so, triggers instinctive rebellion. "Natural Law," precludes the possibility of other reaction.

Bastiat pointed out that people oppressed by excesses of corrupt government will react in one of two ways. They will rebel violently to free themselves from tyrannical injustices, or they will integrate with the system. Integrating with the system means taking on its corruption. This is what has happened to us here in the USA. We've fallen into agreement with taking from each other. We've become a nation of criminals. Everyone wants something for nothing. Everyone steals from everyone. Lacking the courage to fight for freedom as did our progenitors, we have succumbed to slavery. Call us slaves, serfs or whatever you will. The minority who are producers are forced to give the larger portion of their production to the drones.

The drones have become the majority among us. They seek power over the meek through government office or business management or through religious chicanery. This essay would become a fat book if herein were listed all the types of drones and their methods of stripping their supporters of their resources.

The mental capacity of man diminishes with deteriorization of morality. Decadence breeds decadence. We have become like zombies, following each other in the idiotic mores we've developed.

Our religious institutions succumb more each year to the will of the laymen among them. Many of us are still accepting the idea that we have a Creator, or **God**. Most, though, have decided what his rules for them should be. In the wonderful social organizations we call our churches, the desire of paying members is the guiding light. Some let their leaders consider their wishes, then decide what God's will for them should be. Others decide it democratically.

This once great nation of ours is no longer a "Nation Under God". We are now a nation over God. We've created though, not one, but many gods. Every church imputes different attributes and concerns to him. Every person has him accepting their personal pleasures.

The God of old destroyed Sodom and Gomorrah. The Sodomites today have dreamed up a God who either is gay, or, at least accepts them and their degeneracy. Intelligence tells those who will use it, that the God of old, can't be the same god as him whom the Sodomites of today have created for themselves to pray to.

The God of old said we can't serve God and Mammon (money). Today, financial success is the main ingredient for gaining respect among our fellows. Money is unquestionably the most sought after and most esteemed god in our land.

The God of old, commanded his children to multiply and replenish the earth. Today, large families are derided as buffoons. Of course, we can't serve the money god and spend much time and resources on children.

In olden times the people did as we are doing today. They created for themselves a diversity of deity. Like us today, some killed their children, sacrificing them to the God Baal and others. Some ate the sacrifices.

We are more sophisticated. We grind infants to partake of them in the guise of medication and, of course, youth serum. For enough of your money god, you can acquire injections of fetal growth hormones. If you have Parkinsons Disease and money, you can purchase grindings of an unborn baby. The infant of course, had to be killed by a Priest of the money god.

This society does homage to those priests of their money god who experiment with the flesh of their murder victims. Many in this society become incensed if we suggest that the infants are the ones who should have the "right of choice". These degenerates **teach** promiscuity to our youth, then they show them how to try to avoid responsibility for their **taught** illicit behavior-and then they try to justify human sacrifice by claiming the "Right of Choice".

These deviates have to create for themselves, a *God* who can tolerate their actions. A *God* who can allow a woman to choose to make a baby and then have it killed.

Many worship the *God* who allows them to spread deadly disease through sodomy. These claim the right to beguile tender youths. Forget that a **God** of principles would have to allow children to mature before subjecting them to difficult choices, especially choices that will effect their lives and the lives of their entire society.

A "just" **God's** law will have to protect the innocent from the thief and murderer. A "just" **God's** law will have to protect the youth from the Sodomite. A **God** who is fair must provide a "**Law of Liberty**" for all.

The laws of a "just" **God** could not tolerate teaching promiscuity to youth too tender to be capable of handling the results. Nor could His laws promulgate corrupt power by some of His children over others. Neither would His laws allow usurious practices to distribute the wealth from the producers to the drones.

A "just" **God** will not tolerate slavery in any guise. Not in the form of men owning men, nor governments owning their populace. If a government enslaves its people, it is a corrupt government. It is not abiding by the true **God's "Law of Liberty"**.

In nature, all things have opposites. A true **God** must have an opposite. Our true **God**, our Creator, has for his opposite, a unity of all the false *gods* we fools have created. He created us. We create opposition for Him. Probably, at the helm of all this idiocy, there is one master, Anti-**God.**

When the **"Law of Liberty"** is torn asunder and trodden under foot, the people must suffer. This is always the result when **God's** adversary gains the love of the masses. It is easy to see why so many today have become agnostics. What rational being could believe in the *gods* manufactured by this people.

History has proven over and over that evil triumphs over good for periods of time. These time periods always end with great calamities. Let's consider a truism. If a true and just **God** has given to his children a **"Law of Liberty"**, it must be unchangeable. It must be fair for all, in all ages. Logic tells us that a just **God** would do this. Logic tells us also that a just **God** would provide opportunity for his children to receive and practice such a **law**.

If the creation, or children of a just **God**, rebel and corrupt themselves beyond redemption, He must intervene. Beyond redemption means to a point where the **"Law of Liberty"** cannot exist. A point where His **guarantee** of freedom for men becomes invalid. A point where children cannot grow to maturity without evil influences beguiling them into evil and destructive ways.

When societies become this decadent, **God,** if he is just, must destroy them to allow a fresh start. As societies begin anew, at least for a time, freedom can be enjoyed.

If **God** does not take a hand, nature will destroy us utterly. If God will show mercy by at least controlling our destruction somewhat, some of us may survive. If **God** will intervene in our road to self destruction, it is probable that the few uncorrupted will be preserved.

Our fall is imminent. The equal and opposite reaction to breaking of "Natural Law" cannot be stopped. **God** will cut short the time lest the whole earth be destroyed completely. The True **God** cannot change "Natural Law". Your mythical, self- created *gods* could, but they are only myth. Howl you imbeciles. Pray to your dreamed up *deity*. He who is the enemy of **God** uses you only to thwart your Creator. He doesn't cherish you. He uses you only to bring about your own downfall in his eternal struggle against your Maker.

The true **God** demands that we respect our neighbor's rights. He demands that we defend the innocent among us from the criminal. He demands that we stamp out crime on all levels. Only those who are willing to do this deserve a place among free men.

The impending doom that we face can be stopped, we need only to return in sufficient numbers to a decent standard of morality. If enough of us do this, we'll "throw the bums out". We'll re-establish our Constitution, which in it's original form requires justice and freedom for us, the people.

It is the view of the author, that too few men of integrity are left among us. Immorality is too strong. Probably an effort to save our Constitution will be too late. Let's try. If we succeed, how wonderful for our posterity. If we fail, we still can participate in establishing the new order.

As in all ages, after cleansing, or, destruction of corrupt societies, those few who remain will be prone towards establishing **liberty**. After the terrible destruction that will soon come upon the earth, only the honorable men of character will remain; those who will have isolated themselves from the fray; those who will have fled so as to have been free from the need to kill or be killed. This does not mean cowardly flight. It means those who have enough morality that they'll refuse to participate in disorganized carnage.

The author can find no organized church (organized religion) to which he can give fealty. This is not to say that he denies his Maker. He has read into and looked at various faiths. They all put their own twist or interpretation, on what they accept as **God's** word.

While the author can find no group to join with, neither can he deny writings of various proven prophets. The times of great upheaval that we face today have been predicted by many from different walks of life. Seeing the fulfillment of various predictions by men of old, makes reasonable the acceptance of further predictions by them, pertaining to our time.

Presented here is the author's view, from his understanding of natural cause and effect laws. Also his accumulation of wisdom gleaned from the Prophets.

These phenomenon seems to mesh into an understanding that the world's decadence is again destroying itself. Further that the time has come that the morally courageous will truly establish and promulgate **God's "Law of Liberty"**.

A society will emerge wherein greed will be unnecessary. Greed such as is the norm today, results largely from lack of security, such as we have today.

The earth was given by **God** the Creator to his children. No one has a right to usurp, or control the land that belongs to us all. The American Indians have far greater understanding in this area than do we who are supposedly so knowledgeable. With relatively little education, they put our greatest wise men to shame.

The Mexican Agrarian System recognizes the right of the citizen to, use and own enough land to support his family's needs. The USA had homestead laws till power mongers took control and usurped our rights to property. Fail to pay property taxes on your exorbitantly priced holdings today and see how fast the government (no longer your servant) takes your land from you.

In the new order, the State won't own the land as in Communism. Nor will the State lease the land to you and charge taxes perpetually on it, as in the USA. In the coming Utopia, the citizens will be able to claim their rightful inheritance. No one will be able to tax it or get it from them on any other pretext.

In this coming world, men will cherish their families and will support them. Of course, the fruits of men's labor will not be confiscated till they break under the excessive load. They will find it possible to provide for their own. Men won't molest their children, because the very few who try will be executed as quickly as they're discovered.

The criminal will have no place in the new society. The innocent will be protected. The thief will pay dearly. The murderer will cease to exist as will all who prove to honorable judges that they cannot become law abiding citizens.

Men will be independent and will govern their own families. Traits of high moral character will be the prerequisites for anyone seeking the few public offices.

In this society, you will worship whom and how you please. It will be no one's business but your own while your Deity doesn't instruct you to infringe on your neighbor's rights. Worship whom you please, but keep the **"Law of liberty"**.

Among this vast array of hundreds of millions of people, a few million must exist who love the **"Law of Liberty"**. They will band together at the hour of destruction. They will find a place to flee to in order to keep themselves clean, in order to protect their families, and in order to live to fight another day for truth and right.

Watch for the establishment of a **City of Peace**. It will be established. Men of honor will seek each other and unite and will be free. This is nature's law.

Left behind will be the whoremongers, the Sodomites, the murderers, and those who cannot face making their own way with no hope of gleaning from the labor of their fellows. These will remain to die of plagues of their own making, or maybe by the fires they'll set, or by tempest brought by the Supreme Judge.

How horrible for those who can't come to the standard of justice that will be required in the new society. How wonderful for those who can. They will help build a brand new free world. They will re-establish the laws of our fathers. **"The Perfect Law of Liberty."**

Where will you be reader?

End of Essay 10

CHAPTER 2

In the aftermath of the bombings in Oklahoma City, it is hoped that a few more of my countrymen may be amenable to the truth. At least more of us will reflect more seriously than ever on our state of affairs, the condition of our nation. Who can still say "all is well" after the WACO Texas murders and the Oklahoma City massacre?

Those who believe that *all is well*, have been insulated from hardship or are steeped in the idea that their church or religion has **God's** approval and will therefore protect them. Please remember the scripture: ***God** is no respecter of persons.* [1] You are advised here and now that all can be well, only for those who merit **God's** protection through their own actions.

Granted, that acceptance of, or belief in certain religious principles, may position one into a deserving attitude. Surface acceptance though, does not constitute true belief. For instance, many Christians believe that acceptance of Christ as their Savior will bring them salvation. The New Testament seems to partially back this up. It should be remembered though, that: *He that saith I know him, and keepeth not his **commandments** is a liar. The **truth** is **not** in him*[2]. Apparently simple acceptance is not sufficient. It is evident from the scriptures that the keeping of the **Commandments** is a **necessary requisite** to true acceptance.

If scriptures seem to conflict or disagree with one another, it is the interpretation that is faulty. If you can't see this, further reading of this treatise will, for you, be a waste of time.

The author repeatedly reminds the reader that he is not affiliated with any organized church. He has looked at several, but can join none of them. Most put meanings to holy writ that back up their pet concepts while causing a need to ignore other scripture.

No one can refute the fact that the many hundreds of sects would unite if they could agree on doctrinal interpretation. The one belief that does seem common among the religious element here in these United States is that: *All is well.* Although they admit that things are out of kilter, most are sure that they have the

---

[1] II Cronicles 19:7 & Acts 10:34
[2] I John 2:4

Lord on their side and are so favored of him that their problems will right themselves.

In Christendom, the general consensus is that all sin is forgiven if we will accept Christ. Based on this, it must follow that the vast number of Christians are forgiven by the grace of **God**. Forgiven by **God** for their crimes, and therefore, accepted into his society with his protection. Could a "just" **God** bring destruction on a people that have accepted his Christ and received forgiveness for their crimes?

Many who consider themselves to be the only true Christians see the Christ as the supreme **God**. Can it be possible that he would allow destruction to befall a people that accepts his Deity? Again, please read 1 John, verses 2-4 (He that saith I know him and keepeth not his **commandments** is a liar.)

If the Bible says what it means and means what it says, how can this be ignored. When interpretations of other scripture seem to disagree with 1 John, verses 2-4, something is amiss. Either this scripture is false or some others are false or some interpretation is incorrect.

The author writes to his nation, his people, the United States of America. Most of these people believe in a **God**. The vast majority are Jew or Christian. These are the groups with whom the author has associated. The author has studied the scriptures used by these, the majority of Americans. His studies are not done from the view point of any organized group. He does not have to accept interpretations because of the acceptance or understanding of his church group. He has none.

The studies of the author are independent. He welcomes opinions for consideration. He attempts to base his opinions on truth, rather than on popularity of concepts.

The key to understanding of truth will now be described more concisely than earlier on. This key will be referred to throughout this treatise.

The apostle James said, *If any of you lack wisdom, let him ask of **God**, that giveth to all men liberally, and upbraideth not; and it shall be given him. But let him ask in faith, nothing wavering*[3]. You must first have an open mind and be willing to accept truth even if it disagrees with preconceived notions. You must

---

[3] James 1:5-6

be humble enough to realize that one greater than yourself exists, who can give you understanding.

This is the Key: humble, open-minded prayer, exercised with faith.

Faith, of course, needs development. First you must practice open mindedness, desiring to know, meditation, belief in what seems right. If you practice these, belief will become strong enough to be called faith. If you will pray with an open mind and with faith, **God** has promised to answer and give you the wisdom to recognize the truth.

Unlike many of us, **God** does not lie, nor does the promise preclude any particular group of people. It is made to all mankind, both male and female, but ask in faith, nothing wavering.

Dear reader, if you will use this key, your perceptions will be heightened. You will be enlightened. Your understanding will be enhanced. Your ability to understand the truth will be increased. If desirous of truth and willing to pay the price, you can acquire it. If this takes place, you will place yourself in a very small minority, no matter what your religious affiliation is.

Any of you, dear readers, who have watched T.V. or listened to a radio, understand that sound and sight waves can be generated. Your radio or T.V. must be tuned to receive the proper frequency. Having tuned a radio, you have no problem believing that a variety of wave lengths exist. Is it so difficult then to believe that **God** could emanate something similar?—a frequency or wave length which we can receive if we will but attune ourselves to receive it.

The human mind, and our entire system of nerves and glands, generate and emanate, receivable wave lengths. Receivable by ourselves and anyone close enough and willing to tune in.

We've all experienced thought reception. Surely someone, somewhere has verbalized something you had been thinking. Who knows who first generated the thought. It resonated into the mind or minds that received it. Like a tuning fork resonates sound waves, so does the mind resonate to thought patterns.

Have you ever entered a room that was filled with mirth and laughter? If so, you know that the spirit of laughter is catching. Most everyone close by will feel the levity. Anger and other emotions effect us similarly. We must control ourselves carefully to avoid anger in the face of anger. The stronger emotions, such as love, hate, joy, sorrow, anger or mirth seem to emanate with greater power than others. All feelings, all thought for that matter, transmits outward and can be picked up by a tuned-in receiver.

When the Spirit of **God** descends on a man, he becomes calm and collected. The Spirit reacts upon those who will receive it with the light of pure intelligence.

God promised that in these, the last days, He will put his law into our inward parts and write it in our hearts[4]. He can do this only for those of us who will do our part.

Seek by attuning yourself with **God's** spirit. Humble yourself, pray with real intent, and consciously, will yourself to accept the truth. Use the key to understanding truth and right. If you are willing to do this, the truth will be made known unto you.

Do we really believe these scriptures that most of us read and claim belief in? If so, we must accept the biblical claim that the Spirit of **God** fills heaven and earth[5]. It is not then, so difficult to accept the biblical claim that we all can receive his Spirit. If, as claimed in the Bible, we are created in his image,[6] how could we not have a receiver which can be tuned to receive **God's** spiritual emanations.

Most of your contemporaries prefer acceptance of their peers over almost all else. A few, however, would actually rather be right in truth than to be popular. The author seeks these few. These few will become the reapers who must glean the fields to help save those like unto themselves. A gleaning will be performed to gather those who will accept the truth. The truth is that we have a **God** who created our world and ourselves, and who by **virtue** of the **Creation**, has an absolute right to regulate us and our world.

Hear another truth, dear reader: O Israel, once you become a seeker after truth and right, you will ingest **God's Law**. If **God's Law** is truly written in your heart, you need not fear the reproach (charges) of men, nor their revilings. This promise is made to Israel in Isaiah.[7] This is **God's** promise to protect us from our enemies in the last days if we truly accept and practice His law.

---

[4] Jeremiah 31:33
[5] Jeremiah 23:24
[6] Genesis 1:26, 5:1, 9:6 & James 3:9
[7] Isaiah 51:7

Who is Israel? Israelites are the children of the promise. Israel is made up of the twelve tribes who **God** made covenant to protect, if they would but keep their side of the covenant. Their side was to keep the "**Law of Liberty**" the law, which if kept, will keep any people free.

Most of the inhabitants of the Americas are of the blood of Israel. Of course this family is scattered world-wide. There is, however, a strong concentration of us here in this land. **God** prepared this for us, to be a land choice above all other lands. He promised, though, that it would be blessed only so long as its inhabitants remained righteous.

The children of Israel should not become arrogantly proud of their position as the children of the promise. Yes, it is a wonderful promise, but in a sense, it is made to all mankind. The reasoning for this is that according to the scriptures, anyone who truly accepts **God's Law**, becoming righteous, is grafted or adopted into the family of Israel.

The Jews have been hated and persecuted mostly out of jealousy. Many pretexts are used, many reasons are cited. In truth though, the cause has mostly been jealousy. This jealousy is because Israel and the world have interpreted the scriptures to mean that the Jews are the covenant people. They certainly are, but only in that they are also Israelites.

Remember that the covenant was made with all the house of Israel. Israel is formed of twelve tribes. Judah is but one of those tribes. Israel can be all the world, if the world will accept God's laws. The short of this is that jealousy is stupidity in view of the fact that anyone can become a member of the body of the covenant people by truly accepting **God's Law**.

The "**Perfect Law of Liberty**" is the **law** that **God** originally gave to Moses. That same **law** which **God** promised would be established in our time. He said: *And I will make a new covenant with Israel. Not like I did with their fathers, which covenant they break, but, I will put My **Law** into their Inward parts and write it in their hearts. And I will be their **God** and they will be My people*[8]. This **law** is the **Ten Commandments** with all of its **statutes** and its **judgements.**

This perfect law is very simple. There is throughout Exodus, Leviticus and Deuteronomy, some expanding and expounding of the law. It remains nonetheless, simple enough that any twelve year old child should have no trouble understanding it thoroughly.

---

[8] Jeremia 31:33 & Hebrews 8:10

One requirement of the Law is that it (the Law) be taught to the people. How could the people, in fairness, be made responsible to the Law if they did not know and understand it?

You are advised here dear reader, that our United States Constitution is also a very simple law, speaking that is, of its original form. It has been adulterated by traitorous villains. It hardly resembles its original self. We can, nonetheless, still understand the freedoms we were supposed to have had. Our original Constitution attempted to give us adequate protection against our government to allow us to live God's Law.

We hear these days a good deal of protesting about expressions of faith in public places. We hear of considerable concern about prayer in schools and displays of religious artistic scenes. It is felt by some that these things endanger their concept of: "the separation or church and state." This concept, as put forth today, (since the1960s) was not in the minds of the framers of our Constitution. This is a "Johnny come lately" concept.

It is abundantly clear that the framers of our **glorious Declaration of Independence and our Constitution** were mostly religiously devout men. The first migrations to this country from Europe were done to escape religious persecution. A prime reason for the creation of our **Constitution** was to **guarantee "freedom of religion"**, not the suppression of it.

Decisions of Supreme Court Justices which have infringed on the rights of free religious expression are vilely evil. All decisions made by these so called *justices* must be suspect. The spirit of truth and right, the **Spirit** of **God**, if you will, is not in them.

How could our progenitors put forth our Declaration of Independence with such confidence in its rightness? How could they, with the might of right, declare to the world, that we are endowed by our Creator with inalienable **rights**?— **rights** which include: *life, liberty and the pursuit of happiness*. They could make this declaration because they understood that **God's Law** is a guarantee of freedom to all mankind—all those, that is, who will embrace and practice his **Law**.

Our country and its original laws were fought for and founded by men of **God**. Religious men who knew that only spiritual, righteous men could maintain the freedoms they gave their all for. They never meant religious devoutness to be kept out of our government's operation. On the contrary, the religious men who founded our government envisioned it being operated by religious men like themselves.

Prayer was instituted to precede most solemn governmental affairs. In **God** we Trust was written onto the face of our coins. Many proofs could be cited as well as quotations from those early noblemen of faith and dignity. It would waste my time and yours. The honest truth seeker knows the truth of this. The rest of you will choose your own path. We are powerless to stop you.

Yes, our Benefactors, our forefathers, were concerned about church and state separation. The concern was only that one church should not gain control of government as happened with the Church of England and as happened with the Catholic church in so many cases.

Our forefathers understood the intolerance of men for any who believe differently than themselves. For this reason they made clear and tried to guarantee through law, the **right** to **freedom of religion.** They tried to establish a government that could not be taken over by one church who would, of course, attempt to force us all to her way.

Can you honestly believe that while prayer opens congressional sessions, it should be outlawed in our schools? Absurd! This is nonsensical idiocy. Let Jew, Moslem, Christian and any other faith participate together in supplicating our **God** for his blessings. Let any and all people seek through prayer, **God's** Spirit. Where is this more appropriate than in a place of learning?

In our public schools, of course, we should not allow any particular sect to dominate others. It is the height of arrogance, though, to presume to forbid the seeking of **God's** presence by anyone at any time.

The reasons for these writings are simple and two-fold. The author feels great outrage and despair at the social trends in his homeland. He feels compelled to speak out. He is prepared to wear out his life in an attempt to reach even a few of the honest in heart. He must disseminate that which he believes to be the truth.

Yes, this people must be warned of the impending doom. Secondly, this people must be advised of the alternative that their Creator will provide for them. A place of refuge will be prepared for them to flee to. This as the alternative to taking up the sword against their brother and their neighbor.

The compulsion to warn you, dear reader, would not be so great, if times and conditions were more heartening; this however, is not the case. Our nation is in the throes of terrible criminality. We are on the brink of terrible disaster.

Our government has achieved that which our forefathers so greatly feared. It has so corrupted our Constitution that it is scarcely recognizable as the guarantee of freedom it was meant to be. Our government has become an atrocious, gluttonous tyranny.

Our forebears paid a heavy price to free themselves from a tyranny not nearly so oppressive as is ours today. Our progenitors published to the world a Declaration of Independence. In this document, they declared to all mankind, that we are endowed by our Creator with the right to life, liberty and the pursuit of happiness. How dare the traitorous scoundrels destroy our liberty?

As Bastiat said (not verbatim): "When socialistic governments oppress the people, taking from producers to give to non producers, one of two reactions will result. No.1 The people will rise up to overthrow such a tyranny, or; No.2 The people will fight back by becoming criminal like unto their government.[9]

As a people, we've taken the temporarily easier road. We've followed our government into rank criminality. This is a natural reaction to oppression such as is practiced by our *servants*, our "leaders", our elected officials and their appointed, hired henchmen.

We are a criminal nation. Our government fails to fulfill its only legitimate function, the protection of its innocent, or law-abiding citizens. Our government has allowed and even propagated a myriad of evil, corrupt, unconstitutional laws. Our government extracts our resources to a criminal degree. The masses of the people haven't the means left to fight back through our grossly **polluted legal system**.

Those among us who, through greed, have attained to the loftier positions of wealth and power, do not want change toward legitimate equal opportunity. They, of course, have the "rose garden syndrome." Their pride and self importance tell them that those beneath them, are such, due to lack of ambition or willingness to put forth effort.

The lawyers can't believe that it is not their right to extract huge sums for their time. They charge many times the rate at which most of their clients can

---

[9] The Law p.11

earn the money with which to pay them. They tell themselves that without them, the client would get nothing. In truth, they would get nothing without the client.

Our laws and system have been made by lawyers. They have purposefully made our system so complicated that we need their help for what they call legal matters. In general, lawyers are not the kind of people who will fight for justice. They usually fight, rather, for whatever position will get for themselves, the greatest gain with the least effort. As previously stated, this is their *right*, and how dare a client question their procedure or *wisdom*.

There are few absolutes. There are some honorable lawyers. An old respected judge, long ago, stated that 2% of lawyers might have integrity. The author doubts that one out of a hundred lawyers are decent human beings. The author hopes the number is higher but will expend his efforts to find honor in more fertile fields.

The medical profession is like unto the legal field. Physicians extract exorbitantly from the misery of their fellow men. Under conditions of distress, we seek help from these vultures. Our traditions have us looking up to them as saviors. Not so! Like lawyers, most physicians are motivated primarily by greed. Greed kills righteousness, or decent emotion.

The list goes on. Bankers and insurance moguls fit nicely into the category of the greedy. They produce nothing, yet they look down on those fools who provide them with luxury.

More than 50 percent of our working force is employed by government agencies. These may be military, police forces, city, county, state or federal agencies. In any case, only a few of us are providing that which we all are living from. Isn't it *wonderful* to realize also that the supported live far better than their supporters? They live better and they certainly don't act as though they realize from whence cometh their support.

The author is well aware that most of his contemporaries will disagree with him. Many will be angry at his audacity in failing to accept their greatness. Have they not a right to be proud of their lofty positions? Is it not their intellectual superiority that places them in their high stations?

The author is unconcerned about the scorn of the masses. There have never been, nor will there ever be, but a few truly honorable men and women. You cannot truly love **God** if you do not love His **law**. If His **law** is in your inward parts and written in your heart, you cannot help but love **God**. If you truly love **God**, you are only one of a very few.

God's law is the **Law of Liberty**. It requires that men respect each other's rights. It demands that free men be willing to guarantee freedom to their fellows. It demands that we respect each other's right to prosper in health and happiness.

The author believes that some small portion of his readers will agree with the foregoing. He believes that some few will resolve to gather with others like themselves, to re-establish **Liberty**.

The author has put forth views that will seem radical to most. He presents little back-up reference for his philosophy. The reader is expected to meditate, pray, search his soul, to determine whether he can accept these things as valid. A few of you will do this. Claims of impending doom are contained herein. An avenue of escape is described. If ten men and women will listen and act, this effort will be justified.

A few references are used herein to give to you, dear reader, a little corroborative evidence for consideration. Quotes come mainly from the Bible, which is accepted by most Americans, though interpretation varies greatly. As explained earlier, interpretations of the author are untainted by his church, because he has none.

References from sources other than biblical are used, not because of who wrote them, but for what they say. This is where the reader must use his powers of discernment. It is fervently hoped that you will use the key for discernment of truth and right.

The author is well aware that he cannot possibly understand everything perfectly. He believes though, that his understanding is reasonably accurate based on his use of the key for discernment of truth. If the reader will use the same key, we will draw close together in our comprehension of that which is truth.

The intent of this thesis is not to disagree with, nor to cause dissension with or between, any peoples. This effort would not, in fact be made, were these not such perilous times. Did the author not believe sincerely that terrible destruction is coming upon his people, he would not expend his time writing this message.

The author does believe that his nation is already in its death throes. He believes that these times have been clearly described by the prophets from the beginning of our history. He believes that logic should tell any who carefully observe our national state of affairs that we are writhing and thrashing as we crumble. Earlier on it seemed that we might save ourselves. It looks now as though it would be next to impossible.

It behooves all men to be anxiously engaged in a good cause. The greatest cause that can be espoused today is the salvation, or the gathering out of the honest in heart from amidst the rampant evil.

Those among you who in the core of your being love freedom enough to be willing to grant it to your fellows, must unite. You must separate yourselves from those who would usurp evil authority over you. You must prepare yourselves to help re-establish **justice under law**.

We've become so evil that both nature and our **God** are bound to bring about a cleanup. **God's law**, that conforms perfectly to natural law, requires a fresh start for **Liberty**. Even now, as vile usurpation of our rights is tightening, the cleansing has begun.

These writings began as an attempt to simply point out logically the absence of logic of our times and foolishness of our actions as a nation and a people. Some time has passed since this narrative began. The nation has progressed further on its iniquitous journey. The author has studied more deeply. He can see no redemption for the masses.

Let it be understood that the author would welcome the salvation of all. Logic tells him though, that **God** and nature are "**just**." Logic tells him also that the wicked will perish as promised by the prophets. Logic tells him further, that a glorious city of Zion will be established wherein the **Perfect Law of Liberty** will be in full force and effect.

> Have you had enough of blood and guts?
> Lies and fraud and theft and such?
>
> Why, you can leave this place of strife
> Come! Join with us who value life
>
> We'll build a place where men are free
> Where all men hate iniquity
>
> Where law and order are the rule
> To break our law would take a fool

For Justice will be swift and sure
And criminals will be no more

Because we'll drive them from our land
The Law of Liberty will stand

Whore mongers, child abusers too
will learn their kind of life to rue

Men who beat their wives for sport
Will learn the justice of our court

They'll feel the lash and understand
Defense of innocence, we demand

We'll build Utopia, straight and true
Come brothers, there is much to do

No more will government suppress
The widow and the fatherless

Power mongers will be outcast
Freedom's ensign will fly our mast

The worker won't support the drone
What you produce will be your own

Your faith in man will not be shaken
Your goods will not from you be taken

By banker, lawyer and physician
Insurance goon and politician

God's Perfect Law of Liberty
Will be our law and make us free

*Remember ye the **Law of Moses** My servant, which I commanded unto him at Horeb for all Israel, with the statutes and **judgements.**[10]*

---

[10] Malachi 4:4

Dear reader, you are asked to exert yourself to intense exercise of your intellect. You are asked to do this concurrently with use of the key for discernment of truth and right.

Analyze the **statutes** and **Judgements** contained in **God's Law.** Determine for yourself whether **perfect justice** is not therein contained. Judge for yourself whether or not, implementation of this **law** would establish a Utopia.

Perfect logic cannot be presented here because the author is but a frail mortal, possessing not the gift of prophecy. He posseses the gift of revelation, only to the degree that all men may possess it, only to the degree of his own adroitness in exercising the key for discernment of truth and right. He has no special calling beyond that which he perceives to be the duty of every freedom lover.

The author does have a right to revelation of truth, to the same degree as do you all. He can therefore present, though not perfect, a substantially correct analogy of our state of being, in relation to our exercise of correct principles and/or **law**. He can read and understand, as can you all the basics of the " **Perfect Law of Liberty."** If you will read Exodus, Leviticus & Deuteronomy, you can gain much understanding of **God's Law** and the manner in which it requires that we respect each other's rights.

Giving to man the **"law,"** seems to have been, on **God's** part, an attempt to secure for us the freedoms we hold to be our right. Freedom can only exist under law. At the same time, corrupted law tears down and destroys freedom. It would seem, therefore, that **God's** guarantee is largely dependent on our willingness to maintain and/or defend the **"law"** that He gave us.

CHAPTER 3

Our willingness to allow corruption in government has been our downfall. From the beginning we've been so wrapped up in our own selfish pursuits that we've ignored our **duty** to maintain **just law.**

When one tenet of our **law** imposes injustice, the **law** is **corrupted.** When one tenet of our law, fails to protect the innocent through imposition of **judgement**, the **law** is **corrupted.**

Today, in these United States of America, our government is actively destroying the lives of untold numbers of honest, hard working, decent citizens. Many laws are being created (mainly through precedence) which are totally devoid of justice.

We have become a criminal nation. The greatest danger to us, the citizens, is not from the individual criminal. Our greatest danger now comes from our obese and criminal government, which is no longer government of the people, by the people, for the people.

Our Congress in its cowardice and greed, fears to enact laws that might affect the popularity of its members. The *august bodies* (so termed only by themselves) of Congress, know they must show action to their constituents. They wrangle and jangle, making a great show. They pass very few laws, but they create regulatory agencies (**Gestapos**) and they grant to these **Gestapos**, great and evil power over us.

Remember that the only legitimate function of government is the protection of its people. Remember that ours was formed as a government of the people. That which we now have, that calls itself government, takes from us to fight supposed crime, much more than the traditional criminals steal. This statement will be expounded upon in a later chapter. Here it is sufficient to say that our so-called government uses that which it extorts from us to tighten its control and to perpetuate crimes against us.

If we accept as valid **laws,** the myriad of regulations, enacted by our many **gestapos**, none among us can fail to break their law. The IRS, OSHA, The Dept. of Labor and Industries, the EPA, are only a few of the names which strike fear into the hearts of honest men throughout our land. These agencies are not responsible to higher authority. They regularly poke their phallus into the very heart of our industry and our people.

Remember that **our Constitution was established for the express purpose of defending us, the people, from inevitable corruption in government.**

Remember that **our Constitution was formed largely to protect our rights as set forth in our Declaration of Independence.**

Don't forget that **any and all laws that fail to do the foregoing are unconstitutional.** Don't forget that **any law that is unfair is unconstitutional.**

A law that is unfair or unconstitutional is illegal. Of course legality is defined much differently by your lawyer friends and politicians. Legality, as defined in this writing though, means **justice, fairness and right**. The lawyer description makes legal, any "crap" these traitorous vipers choose to enact for tighter control over us.

The Federal Government is not the only gluttonous rapist we have to contend with. The city, county and state governments are trying to emulate big brother. If you are a producer of goods or services, you are surrounded on all sides by vultures. Every day of every year this "Great Whore" grows stronger. She takes and takes and takes. So many feed from you, that of course, you can never have security. There can never more be anything for the producer beyond a very meager, daily sustenance.

The "Great Whore" must feed and feed she will. She can only feed on us the producers. There is no other sustainable source.

> The people scurry to and fro
> Breaking their backs and wearing out
> So the "Whore" can fat and fatter grow
> So the "Whore" can glory, gloat and shout
>
> And praise herself, and dance and revel
> And defecate on the poor dumb devil
>
> The brute who wields the ax or shovel
> Who does her will and lives in a hovel
>
> And feeds the bitch and sings her praises
> And builds her great and glorious palaces

So, having this powerful, bountiful resource
This brutish, hunchbacked, stupid work force

The "Harlot" can travel the wide world over
And meddle and diddle and exert her power

She'll extol and cajole, but her aim is control
Over every land and knoll and shoal

Of every single living thing
She truly thinks she should be king

She truly thinks that she is Godly
Because she's duped and robbed the lowly

But the worker is tiring of playing the fool
Of existing only for use as her tool

Our rulers have driven us much too far
And soon they'll learn that we really are

The children of a living God
That they can't perpetually prod

And scorn and persecute and goad
And burden with excessive load

Yes soon the shackles we will break
A new, fair system we will make

We'll make new covenant with God
We'll promise not to spare the rod

We will defend each other's right
To **LIBERTY** with all our might

Yes, we'll throw off the slaver's chain
We'll laugh and love and sooth the pain

We'll claim the right they tried to give us
To life, liberty and the pursuit of happiness

Anyone who has experience with the "**Gestapos**" knows that with them, any semblance of the "innocent until proven guilty" concept is lost and gone forever. They seek any excuse to exert their *Lordly* power over us. They have unlimited funds, extracted of course from us.

With our money for their sustenance, they use against us our "*Justice System*" (which we pay for). They impose heavy fines and prison sentences on US Citizens who have injured no one. Our (now **Gestapo** type) *Justice System* aids them every step of the way in destroying the lives of untold numbers of Americans. They impose ridiculously exorbitant fines. Of course, this is the prime purpose. The lie sold to John Q. Public is that they are protecting us. In truth they are stimulated by two motives: extraction of filthy lucre with which to continue financing their evil practices and cementing and increasing their great power over us.

They glory and revel in smashing down and destroying men of honor and decency. The greater the destruction of their fellows, the greater their "high". They are filled with the spirit of evil. They love not the truth. They are so stupid that they fail to see the results of their vile idiocy. They seem not to understand that they are killing the goose that lays the eggs.

In the cases of many innocent violators of the corrupt regulations of the regulatory "**Gestapo**", the fines collected cannot offset the cost. They (servants of **Gestapos**) think they're adding to the fund needed for their own excessive take and perpetuation of their evil. Their minds are so blackened that they can't see beyond their noses. Though heavy fines are often imposed, many simply cannot pay them.

In the following chapters, a few cases will be described for your consideration. Please use the key for determining truth and right in forming your opinion of these cases. Please consider also whether the **prophet Isaiah** was just a kook or was he truly a **Prophet of God?** Many of his prophecies have clearly been fulfilled. Many of them however, clearly pertain to our times and our present condition, and are in the process of fulfillment. The few cases that will be discussed hereafter, typify that which is happening all over our land. In describing us (latter day Israelites) Isaiah said*: 20 Woe unto them that call evil good, and good evil; that put darkness for light, and light for darkness; that put bitter for sweet, and sweet for bitter! 21 Woe unto them that are wise in their own eyes, and prudent in their own sight 22 Woe unto them that are mighty to drink wine, and men of strength to mingle strong drink: 23 Which justify the wicked for reward, and take away the righteousness of the righteous from him 24 Therefore as the fire devoureth the stubble, and the flame consumeth the chaff, so their root* *shall be as rottenness and their blossom shall go up as dust: because they cast away the law of the Lord of hosts, and despised the word of the Holy One of Israel.*[11]

---

[11] Isaiah 5: 20-24

CHAPTER 4

The term "cultist" must be defined because it is used to justify evil and even murderous acts by our government. A favorite term among the pious as well as the media is "cultist." This word according to Webster, simply describes a religious organization. Webster goes so far as to call it religious snobbery, but more precisely, a system of religious worship.

The term as used by the media and by the pious, seems to be more closely related to a religious group from which one cannot easily escape. It also seems to be reserved among the pious, for groups with beliefs which differ from those of the group defining the "cultist"

The author has been told, for example, by both Lutherans and by Born again Pentecostal Christians, that Jehovah's Witnesses and Mormons are two of the great "cults." The concept of Deity it seems, differs between Witnesses, Mormons and these other all-knowing groups.

It is wonderful for them that they're able to separate those scriptures they like from those that oppose their view. It is wonderful for them that they can achieve honor and glory in their own minds by condemning these horrible cultists. The author has heard certain Mormon fundamentalist groups described by main stream Mormons as cults.

The media called Koresh and his Branch Davidians cultists. It seems that they were putting forth the "cult" meaning which describes people who are tied very tightly to their organization. In this context, "cult " seems to mean that people through brain washing or otherwise have great difficulty in leaving the organization.

It is interesting to note that "cult" does seem to have different meaning to different people. It is also interesting that it seems not to matter so much if injustice is done to people of a "cult." They probably don't deserve protection under our Constitution anyway. Don't you agree?

It is felt that you should remember the Waco Texas massacre as one of the cases presented here for your scrutiny. Little will be said about that case as you all have had ample opportunity to study it. It has been made very public. Mostly of course, from the point of view of the government. What did you expect? Did you think you'd see witnesses from the Davidian side of the fence? Of course you didn't. You did get to see the very young girl whose mother was killed, whose father and sole support, obviously hated them and who damn sure told the story the government wanted you to hear.

The author believes that the Waco fiasco was cold blooded murder of the very worse kind. This was murder of numerous innocent people by an agency of our own government. An agency that supposedly was formed for protection of our citizens.

The author does not believe that one single aspect of the freedom of his countrymen was infringed upon by the Branch Davidians. The BATF very apparently attempted to attain to glory and praise from the public, and more importantly, from those in authority over them. So hungry were they for this glory, that they were totally blinded to truth and right.

The BATF certainly did commit one of the most heinous crimes of all time. In continuing to persecute the survivors, all who participate make themselves party to this horrible injustice. Our government, including every individual, who in any way, goes along with persecuting the survivors or exonerating (failing to punish) the perpetrators is grossly criminal.

Please read the book titled: The Ashes of Waco". Judge for yourself. For our purposes at this time, you are simply asked to consider very carefully whether the government had a right to kill those children no matter what kind of person Koresh may or may not have been. You are asked also to remember that it is an utter impossibility for you ever to get an entirely true story from the news media. The Davidians were a "Cult", but not in the context as put forth by the media. They were simply a devoutly religious church organization.

There may even be someone in the vast expanse of the media world that wants to get the truth out to the public. Mostly they care only about producing information intriguing enough to pique your interest. If an isolated individual wants to tell the truth, there isn't time to sift the facts to determine the right from the wrong.

The news is enhanced with lies. Outright lies are told on a regular basis. It is nothing but an attention-getting show. Its purpose is to sell advertisements. Our society is fascinated by the news. It is hoped that some of you at least can see through it.

The Waco massacre should be studied by all Americans. It has been well described in the book, "The Ashes of Waco" by the courageous, Dick J. Reavis. This vile crime is apparently going unpunished by our Government. Remember

71

that the only legitimate function of government is protection of its law abiding citizens.

The Davidians appear to have been completely innocent of crimes which should have invoked the use of force against them. Force was used by an agency of our government to the extent of horribly murdering these innocent people. Should we now quake in our boots and call our government righteous? A government that will participate in this kind of atrocity will surely pay a heavy price in the long run.

The first case that will herein be discussed in depth, is that of Bruce Alan Kirschman. He was illegally charged by the District Attorney from Sacramento, California. He was imprisoned in El Paso, Texas, pending extradition to Sacramento.

The author feels to insert here a breif statement pertaining to his relationship or lack of relationship with Kirschman. The author never met the man till he was asked to visit him in the El Paso County Jail. The visit was made and also aquaintence was established with Kirschman's wife, Tracy Johnson from whom most of the Kirschman story was gleaned. Tracy Johnson supplied copies of letters and court transcripts to the author along with her telling the story.

If the Kirschman story gives the impression that it may have been written as a result of friendship or intimacy between Bruce A. Kirschman and the author, the impression will be false. A surface friendship did develope through the author's study of Kirshman's problems and later through breif visits while Kirchman was out on bail in El Paso. No friendship exists between Kirschman and the author due to differences that became apparent through the breif aquaintenceship. No further expanation is offered because it could have no bearing on the following true story which is included here as an example of the gross injustice that is prevalent throughout our land.

Kirschman seems to be what most of us would call a religious Zealot. He can't be labeled cultist because he hasn't a church to affiliate with. It wouldn't help him if he were a cultist. We've seen that at least the small cults have not the protection supposedly afforded by our constitution.

Cults as large as the Jehovah's Witnesses or the Mormons have too large a tax base. It would be unwise to eliminate that many tax payers. We know, however, that small cults don't give us protection, at least from our government.

Bruce Kirschman in any event has not the protection of any group. He's a loner. Kirschman was in prison in El Paso, Texas as this manuscript was prepared. His background is Mormonism. His problems stem from his foolishly studying the books containing the doctrines of the Mormon people; the foundation, if you will, or that which went into the creating of this religious society.

This man, Bruce Kirschman, accepted as gospel, the written word, or the doctrines of his church's founders. This could be considered foolishness by many of his fellows, because, of course, it caused his excommunication and made him an outcast and a loner.

Like most churches, the Mormons teach their followers that certain actions will bring the blessings of God. Like most churches, the greatest blessings are acclaimed as spiritual.

The Mormons go so far as to teach their people that life is eternal and that man can progress eternally if he will conform to the requirements. They cite statements of their Christ. Like all religious groups, members of the hierarchy interpret His (Christ's) statements for their followers.

The Mormon (LDS) leaders teach their followers that the "Gospel" is eternal. The old timers taught very emphatically that the laws of **God**, are the same in all ages of the world, for all people. According to them, you can't have Abraham's blessings if you don't live Abraham's **law**. According to them (old time Mormons), you cannot please **"Father God"** unless you practice the same religion and receive the same ordinances as did the prophets of old. This sounds all right doesn't it?

Surely no one will find fault with this doctrine, the call to live according to the teachings of the scriptures as explained by the "Prophets". The youth in Mormondom (the pious among them, that is) glory in the knowledge that they are able to please their God. Certainly the pleasing of our God is a worthy desire. If we all would do so, our world would surely be a Utopia. The youth of Mormondom have no exclusive though, on the desire to please God. The desire of the religious element, throughout the world, is to teach their youth to love God and please him by complying with his desires (requirements).

Why do you think that Christ told the people to become as little children? He said that of such is the Kingdom of Heaven[12]. Children are teachable, moldable,

---

[12] Matthew 19:14

pliable. They easily develop faith. *Give me your children young enough*, said a great pope *and I'll make Catholics of them forever.*

Now hear this! Most churches believe as do Mormons, that they are in compliance with God's rules. We could discuss many of them, but it is not the intent of this writing. The author couldn't care less about pointing out the differences of opinion among the hundreds of religious groups. One common belief is presented: **most of you do believe that the only way to heaven is through your own church, or at least through your concept of scriptures.**

This digression is merely to remind you that the Mormons have no exclusivity on their attempt to control their membership from childhood forward. Most of you do it. There is certainly nothing wrong with it to the degree that you teach truth. When you use this principle to teach intolerance though, remember that you will reap what you sow.

The Mormon Society spends a great deal of their time in religiosity. A good Mormon places his religion first in his life. In other words, the most important thing in his life is compliance with God's desires (for most of them, of course, as explained by church leaders). The Mormon youth spend much of their time in church and other Mormon society functions. In contrast to days of yore, the time is not spent in study of scripture, nor study of their roots.

Meetings are more in the nature of social gatherings. Of course they still study some Gospel. It's done though from a contemporary viewpoint. If followers question differences from the old ways, they are assured that there is no need to bother their head, they have living prophets to guide them.

This becomes somewhat problematic when some are blessed with greater intelligence, or maybe it's just a stronger desire to know for certain. Maybe it's a stronger bent toward freedom of thought. In any event, the Mormon church, like most church organizations, undergoes constant change. The changes are similar to those of other church groups. The parent church changes or deviates from that which they had held to be God's laws. Individuals or splinter groups who don't believe men can change **God's** laws, either pull, or are driven away. They become reformed or fundamentalist groups. These groups usually try to uphold the "old laws"

Those who've remained faithful to the mainstream Mormon church, going along with the changes, are a closely knit society. Most will follow the leader without question. Most hate and persecute fundamentalists, considering them to be bitter enemies.

Let's recap a little. The Mormons used to teach their people from childhood that the gospel, the ordinances thereof, and the offices to officiate and perform the ordinances, are and have always been and will always be the same. They can no longer encourage deep study of the scriptures, as this will show their present teachings to be inconsistent with the **"Always the same"** concept. The people have too much knowledge to allow burning of the books. The Mormon hierarchy has no choice but to cease teaching the **"always the same" doctrine.**

They must also continue their present policy of **not** encouraging study of the old ways. They must continue to stress the idea that they have **living Prophets,** so the people really needn't worry about seeming differences between old teachings (scripture) and present ideology.

Under present policy, the Mormon church needn't worry about heavy losses to the Fundamentalists, the splinter groups who couldn't turn off beliefs in the **Prophets.** These people have the audacity to ask the living **prophets** for some prophecy. What rank disloyalty. Few people of this ilk are being produced under the current church policies. Not many will learn about their old time religion anymore.

God commands through a **prophet.** Men change the law to conform with the wishes of the people. These damn fundamentalists have the gall to stick with what they perceive to be **God's** wishes. It's no wonder, is it, that the Mormon church, excommunicates, hates and persecutes these rebels.

It is hoped dear reader, that you will have sufficient perception to realize that the intent here is **not** to sell Mormon Fundamentalism. The intent of this segment of this thesis is to point out the inhumanity of man to man, in this case the Mormons to their own. It appears to the author, that the Mormon people hate and persecute more than any other people, their own, for accepting that which Mormon doctrine teaches and demands.

The Mormon people destroy the lives of their own, if they accept what Mormon Doctrine sets forth as **God's** laws. The author saw this persecution first hand in his youth. He didn't realize till now, that it is as alive as ever.

Many tenets of Mormonism have been dropped. Many requirements of their faith either have been done away or are simply ignored, not stressed, or taught about. It is now a religion that nicely fits the desires of its people.

This religion truly makes no tough demands on its membership nor does it require anything that could invite criticism from the rest of the world. It fits nicely into the mold of acceptable behavior for our latter-day, national society.

It seems that mainstream Mormons greatly fear that they may be confused with fundamentalists. They (mainstreamers) will do anything to achieve the good will of their compatriots. They most certainly abolished, as requirements of their church, that which they previously held up as **laws** of **God**. They most certainly did this, specifically and precisely, to purchase the goodwill of their national compatriots.

We cannot condemn the Mormon people for doing what most religious groups throughout history have done. The author at least believes that inherent in our inalienable, **God given rights**, was the right of the Mormons to reject that which they had previously claimed to be **God's** laws. They have, in the author's view, a right to do anything they wish, excluding only, infringement on the **rights of others**.

Yes, they had a legal right to change their laws, break their covenants and to turn traitor to their founders. They do not, however, have a right to persecute those who choose to pursue the living of **God's laws**, as they see them.

In preparation for this work, the author has studied some of what the Mormons still proclaim as their doctrine. Understand now, that a main tenet of this people is the acceptance and upholding of the "Law of the Land." This church regulation is necessarily stressed very strongly. This is their out. This is how they justify doing away with tenets established by their early **Prophets** as **laws**.

It is put to you. You are asked to judge. Can it possibly be that the requirement to obey the "Law of the Land" should supersede the **Law** of **God**? So that you, dear reader, may more fully understand Mormon philosophy in this regard, some quoting from their doctrine will be done and a little of their history will be presented. Please decide for yourself whether they uphold our **God given freedoms** or, whether they've simply united with our government in usurping wicked tyrannical authority over their own people.

The "Doctrine and Covenants" is published by the Mormon Church. It is acclaimed by them as being mostly revelation from **God**, or Christ, through Joseph Smith, Jr., the **Prophet**. The 98th section of the Doctrine and Covenants purports to be the word of **God**. Verses 4 through 11 are quoted.

Verse 4: *And now verily I say unto you concerning the law of the land, It is my will that my people should observe to uphold all things whatsoever I command them. 5: And that law of the land which is constitutional, supporting that principle of freedom in maintaining rights and privileges, belongs to all mankind and is justifiable before me. 6: Therefore, I the Lord, justify you, and your brethren of my church in befriending that law which is the* **constitutional law** *of the land. 7: And as pertaining to the law of man, whatsoever is more or less than this cometh of evil. 8:* **I the Lord God** *make you free, therefore you are free indeed; and the law also maketh you free. 9: Nevertheless, when the wicked rule, the people mourn. 10: Wherefore, honest men and wise men should be sought after diligently, and good men and wise men you should observe to uphold; otherwise whatsoever is less than these cometh of evil. 11: And I give unto you a commandment, that ye shall forsake all evil and cleave unto all good, that ye shall live by every word which proceedeth forth out of the mouth of God.*

This sounds pretty good. Who could argue with it? How could anyone twist this to mean that **God** requires compliance with the law of the land without qualification. The **God** in whom the first Mormons believed, justified their obeying **constitutional law**. He justified **righteous law**. He commanded them to forsake evil law and evil administrators. Could anything be more clear?

Can you see now why Mormon leadership cannot have the laymen studying and understanding their **old laws**? How could they require an informed people to comply with law of the land that has become evil? They couldn't. No one could require this of an informed public.

Now comes the great separator. Now comes the history that requires of you, dear reader, exercise of the key for understanding truth. If you continue reading here, you either must be capable of tolerance for other's beliefs, or you will become hateful toward these writings and the author.

A law was given to the Mormon people, according to their published doctrines, a law given by **God** through a **Prophet.** This law according to their **Prophet,** was the same as was lived by Abraham, Sarah and Hagar of old. The Mormon **Prophet,** called it the **Law** of Sarah. The Mormon people accepted this and practiced the **Law** of Sarah (polygamy) until 1890.

The Mormons were hated, persecuted, driven by their countrymen. Many wild stories were invented about them. This can't be hard to believe. Every religious sect in existence has false concepts about all other religious sects.

Of course the Mormons were criticized and hated. Their beliefs were very radical and different from the norm. They went so far as to claim revelation directly from **God**. They claimed present-day revelation. How outrageously absurd this sounded to non-believers and it still does. Polygamy was one of the tenets of the Mormon Faith that was vigorously attacked by their contemporaries. The author believes that polygamy was a scapegoat.

If you hate someone enough to seek occasion against him, you'll try to find something in his actions to attack. In the days that the Mormons were a hated people, the polygamy issue became the cohesive element to unite the country against them. It is probable that more people than not would have been unconcerned about the size of a man's family, had they not needed something for which to hate Mormons.

No! It is not felt that most of the people would have practiced polygamy. Most though, would have been tolerant of their neighbor's beliefs as long as their own rights were not infringed upon. They could not, though, be tolerant, because, these were the hated Mormons.

The Constitution of the United States of America guarantees religious freedom to citizens of the states included in the union. The territories on the other hand, had no such guarantee.

The U. S. Congress outlawed the practice of polygamy in the territories. They then refused statehood to Utah, agreeing to allow it if the Mormons would abolish the controversial practice.

The Mormons were tired of persecution. They preferred statehood over keeping that which they had accepted as God's law. They purchased their statehood. The Utah legislature (at that time controlled by mormons) in establishing Utah's constitution, therein forbade bigamy.

Yes, many states have passed laws prohibiting bigamy. Bigamy, that is, being defined as a man being legally married to two women at the same time.

If laws anywhere prohibit extra marital affairs, these laws are a well kept secret. It seems, from a legal stand point at least, that this is all right. Multiple girl friends, or multiple mistresses, even for married men, seems to be acceptable to most. At least it's not criminally illegal (except, maybe in the Mormon state of Utah).

Now hear this! Laws enacted by states, against bigamy, at least bigamy practiced on the basis of one's religious beliefs, are "Green River Laws." A "Green River Law" is a law that is **unconstitutional.**

Logic tells us of course, that if the 1st Amendment[13] means anything, laws cannot be passed which interfere with our right to free exercise of our religion. One need not be a mental giant to understand this. Are you determined to feign ignorance? Do you lack the ability to accept the idea that the 1st Amendment says what it means and means what it says? If so, you are very well qualified to sit as a Supreme Court judge.

Most Americans think bigamy or polygamy is illegal. This is false. What is illegal is a law that forbids bigamy or polygamy, at least when practiced under religious conviction. You understand, of course, that this means legal according to **Constitutional Law**. Most decisions have gone against polygamy because most *justices* have based decisions on their own concepts of morality rather than on **Constitutional Law**. It is too bad that men whose concept of morality dissagrees with that of the holy men of the Bible, should have power over us and power to interpret our glorious **Constitution** according to their own concepts.

Are you thinking that the author advocates polygamy? Well he does not. The author advocates neither polygamy or monogamy. It is none of his business how anyone conducts their life, so long as they don't infringe on the rights of others. If men and women choose to unite in honorable marriage, raising their children in a clean family environment, why should anyone oppose them?

Of course, the carnal and devilish nature of man drives him to meddle in the affairs of others. Few of us can be truly tolerant of views other than our own.

From the time that the Mormons agreed to blend in with mainstream America ideology-wise, they've been free of persecution. They still have the persecution complex but, in truth, suffer no more intolerance than do most religious groups, from those whose beliefs do not agree perfectly with their own.

Yes! Catholics, Baptists, Methodists, Pentecostal, Born Again Christians and all the rest, sneer at and belittle Mormons. They do this to each other also and so do Mormons sneer at them, while gloating over their own superiority.

The Mormons of course, left themselves wide open to criticism. When they abolished what they claimed were their **God's Commandments**, they invited

---

[13] 1st amendment to the US Constitution

scorn from the masses. They had to either be wrong in the first place, or wrong in abandoning this most serious tenet of their faith. If it was wrong to begin with, they started out immorally and built their foundation on that immorality. If it was right to begin with, then they were cowards for giving it up.

As a religious belief, polygamy has never been illegal under the U.S. Constitution. Unconstitutional laws have been passed against the practice. Could this be justifiable grounds for a people to give up what they believe to be a requirement of their **God**?

If you are a Mormon with a persecution complex you will consider this writing to be such. Remember please, that no action against you is herein suggested for your beliefs, or lack of them. The author cannot feel that speaking out against ideologies or actions can be properly construed as persecution, especially if only truth is spoken.

That for which the Mormon people do deserve harsh punishment has nothing to do with their beliefs. Their willingness as a people to persecute and destroy the lives of their own earns them a deserved place among the vilest of criminals. They, the Mormons, have themselves passed illegal laws (unconstitutional) with which to prosecute, incarcerate and break up countless families.

In their cowardice, they turned traitor to their founders and their doctrines. They then turned to making war on any of their own who remained loyal to or regained loyalty for their most cherished principles.

No intelligent person could study deeply into Mormonism without forming the following analogy: Either their founders were wrong and fostered a great hoax on this people or; their founders were right and spoke for **God**.

If the Mormon founders were wrong and this people have built their society and ideology on false premises from the beginning, what can they have now? Better for them if this is the case, for if their founders were right, and truly spoke **God's** commands, where are this people now?

If their founders spoke truth, then this people have unquestionably, "changed the law and broken the everlasting covenant." What a predicament for a people, who in general, want to do good. It is pretty tough for people to overcome the traditions of their fathers.

For the sake of decency, a plea is extended to the Mormon people. "Let my people go." Open your prisons, free those whom you're persecuting for pursuing that which they believe to be the **will** of **God**. Honor their **constitutional right to freedom of religion.**

Enough has been said about this people who were certainly within their rights in abandoning or changing their **law**. They certainly have as much right to reject their laws as to accept them. Our God-given **LIBERTY** does give us all **free agency**.

The author's sister, after reading this manuscript commented that it sounds hateful of the LDS (Mormon people). It is not meant to sound that way, nor is it the case. The author was raised in Mormondom. He has, among that people, many dear friends and much beloved family. It is hoped that the reader can differentiate between outrage at injustice and love and respect for the honest in heart, the tolerant among the LDS (Mormon) people who **love justice**. Many among them are fine people who would not knowingly accept intolerence and injustice. The author reiterates his sworn statement that this is an indictmemnt only of those among that people who deserve it. They know who they are.

Before returning to the **Kirschman Story,** just a little more must be discussed about this controversial system of family government that is so hated by mainstream Mormons.

Clearly, the practice of polygamy, when done through a sense of religious duty, is perfectly legal. Any who contest this, do so out of ignorance, prejudice or just plain maliciousness.

Let's analyze this controversial religious tenet in the context of morality. First it seems appropriate to determine from whence cometh our mores or our concepts of that which is or is not moral. Among you, dear readers, may be differing opinions. You are all entitled to your own.

Webster's dictionary defines "morality" as ethics, upright conduct, conduct or attitude judged from the moral standpoint. Webster describes "moral" as an adjective, concerned with right and wrong and the difference between them, that which is "moral" being the right.

The author has found nothing to use as an authoritative guideline except Biblical Scripture. This is where right and wrong, good and bad and ethics are outlined.

Probably, most of you will agree that compliance with the **Law of Moses** does constitute morality. A summary of the **Law of Moses** is universally known as the **Ten Commandments.** Yes, the **law** does include a little more than that found in the summary. It is simple still. It is found throughout the Old and New Testaments. It is possible though, to find a substantially complete outline of **God's law (the Law of Moses)** in Exodus, Leviticus and Deuteronomy.

One must remember that Moses descended both genetically and ideologically from Abraham. Abraham walked and talked with **God.** He received great promises from **God,** The greatest of which was that he would be held as father to all the righteous, from his time forward.

Think ye that **God** considered Abraham to be immoral? Think ye that **God** would have named Abraham, the father of all righteous, if he were an immoral man? Absurd! If you know anything about Abraham, you know he was a polygamist.

The "**Law of Moses**" is **God's Law.** It was given through Moses the **Prophet.** Please consider the following biblical scriptures:

If a man has a wife, and taketh another, he shall not diminish the support of the first, nor his husbandly duties to her.[14] (**God's law** to Israel).

If a man lay with a maid, he shall surely marry her.[15] (**God's law** to Israel) This law was **not** prefaced with "unless he has a wife already."

There is ample evidence throughout Holy Writ, that plurality of wives is not considered by **God** (the author of morality) to be in any way immoral. The holy men and women of old were polygamists.

The author is not a polygamist, but will defend to the death, the rights of all men to exercise their **God-given, Constitutional, moral freedom.** Bruce Alan Kirschman was a Mormon. Not too good a one, because he had the audacity to study deeply, his church's doctrines. He became convinced that the written word was right over the living prophets who never prophesy.

Bruce's wife Julie felt the same way that he did. Their **God** required extra sacrifice from them. They believed that they were supposed to live like the holy ones of old. In Mormondom, this happens occasionally. Unsuspecting *fools* continue to drink deeply of their **God's** word, as they see it, through Mormon founders.

---

[14] Exodus 21:10
[15] Exodus 22:16

Now and then someone trips and is caught up in what they consider to be a testimony of the truth. Many develop a burning belief (testimony) that they have a duty to observe to uphold **God's laws** as they see them. Some actually do so.

Now we all know that throughout our land, many practice polygamy or similarly take various mistresses. It is generally frowned upon, but is really, for the most part, accepted as "their own business." Of course, most of us dislike it if we get stuck with supporting the children through welfare. If they provide for their own though, most of us feel that it is not our concern. Not so in Mormondom.

Mormons hate, subjugate, persecute and prosecute with zeal (through illegal laws), anyone who dares to accept Mormon doctrine in contrast to mainstream Mormon practices. How dare these Daniels[16] Meshak, Shadrach and Abednigoes[17] have the courage to practice the laws of God that we rejected? Off with their heads! Into the lions den! Into the fiery furnace! At least throw them into a dungeon.

Many, many men have spent many, many years, imprisoned for having lived polygamy in Utah. Elmer Kelch spent twenty-seven years behind bars. As each five-year sentence ended, he went back to the families he loved. Each time he did so he was sent back to prison.

> Oh what anguish you will see
> If justice truly is to be
>
> If we truly reap that which we sow,
> You who bring the righteous low
>
> Will rue the day you persecuted
> Men of honor, who were faultless

In recent years, it has become more difficult even in Mormondom to jail men for taking more than one wife. Partially because the Constitution of the United States protects religious freedom. Partially because men of intelligence know that before **God**, a marriage need not have men's stamp of legality on it to be valid.

---

[16] Daniel 6:10
[17] Daniel 3: 1-23

Knowing that they can incur the wrath of corrupt, religious, fanatical contemporaries and corrupt law officials, wise men and women act wisely. Most polygamists do not make the mistake of having legal ceremonies performed. They may find a Priest of their faith, or they may make their vows personally to each other, before their **God**.

Mostly they are aware that, if as they believe, they are acting righteously, that evil must surely rise up against them. Out of simple preservation, most of them wisely do not, in the eyes of the *law*, become polygamists. The *law* cannot, even illegally attack a man who has only one legal wife (one civil marriage).

This was the case with Bruce Kirschman. He and Julie were converted. They met others like themselves who had also become converted. They entered into plural marriage. Tracy Johnson, a good Mormon girl, entered their family under a condition of "common law." Tracy was converted to plural marriage. She fell in love with Bruce. Julie and Bruce both wanted her in their family. Since the repeal, in the late 1970's, of the un-constitutional, Edmunds Tucker Law, this was perfectly legal by all standards.

Imagine the consternation of their families. This put them in opposition to the *living Prophets* (who don't prophesy) and on outs with all good and dutiful Mormons. In this closely knit society, they became outcasts, evil doers. Their friends, the families they loved, their church leaders, all turned on them. How lonely this must be.

They couldn't nail this evil man legally. Remember that he was wise enough to have only one legal, civil marriage.

Who can say what causes alienation of affection in a loving wife? No two are alike. Suffice it to say that after a couple of years or so of polygamy, Julie changed her mind. The poor woman must have had tremendous pressure from her family and friends from the beginning.

Julie must be a greatly virtuous and unselfish woman. She has born ten children. She freely entered into what she believed to be the **"Law of Sarah."** Honor and praise should be heaped upon her. It could not possibly be, though, in Mormondom. She must have suffered greatly at the disgust and revulsion of her family and friends. What woman does not cherish the good will of those around her?

Whatever her reasons, Julie decided to get out of the relationship. She had as much right to get out as she'd had to enter into this marriage system.

That which is not right, is that the husband and father should lose all rights to his children because she changed her mind. Separation or divorce is sad. It is sometimes necessary. Usually, both mother and father should have equal rights to parent the children. This is usually best for the children. Unless one parent is unfit and will somehow damage the children, there can be no justification for legal meddling to allow other than equal and joint rights.

Consider now what happened in Mormondom to this *evil* polygamist. Julie fled with the children from their home in Utah to Wilton, California. This is in Sacramento County. You couldn't exactly call Sacramento County Mormondom, but if everyone there with whom you had to deal were Mormons, you probably would feel that you were in Mormondom. If you were required to seek justice from Mormon officials of the *law*, who couldn't care less about the legality of your position because you are a polygamist, you would certainly feel that you were in Mormondom.

The law gives California jurisdiction over children (right to establish custody rights, etc.) after six months of residency. In other words, until children are residents in California for the prescribed time, the state has no legal right to interfere with a parent's custody rights. Remember now, that the officials who **illegally** involved themselves in this case were devout Mormons. We *shouldn't expect* them (though officers of the court), to act within legal bounds, should we? Of course not, they were Mormons and therefore considered themselves to be above the laws the rest of us are subject to. Besides they were dealing with a hated polygamist.

Kirschman's children were taken without his knowledge or consent to the home of his father-in-law in Wilton, California. Living in this home, was Julie's brother, Paul Renee Goffaux, a convicted child molester. We are told by our experts that child molesters do not cease their vile activities. If justice were to be done, child molesters would be summarily executed. In our cowardice in this nation, we slap their hands and send them back to enjoy our children some more. Some communities have had the commendable courage to forbid residence to convicted child molesters.

Julie, on the other hand, took her nine children (one had died soon after birth), to live with a molester. Her parents, the Goffaux's went along and helped her with this. Her parent's pastor (Mormon Bishop), helped her and her parents' with this. The Sacramento courts gave Julie legal custody. They had no legal right to do so. Not only were the children not legal (six month) residents, but they were not even in the state of California when the illegal custody order was issued. They were at that time with their father in the state of Utah.

What difference should that make? The investigator who is also the officer that arrested Bruce is a devout Mormon. Kirschman is on the Mormon hate list. Why should this *honorable* (Mormon) officer operate within the law? Why shouldn't he help his Mormon cronies railroad this hateful polygamist?

They issued an illegal custody order after the children (never legally under their jurisdiction) had left the State. For good measure they also charged him with burglary for taking his violin, an inheritance from his grandfather. It was in the house into which he had been invited by his children.

In truth, we know that he would have been an unfit father, had he acted **differently** than he did. What decent man would leave his children in a dangerous environment? Even had corrupt *laws* opposed his taking his children; duty and decency would have demanded that he take them. He had, however, every legal right to take them, as well as his duty.

The illegality is solely on the part of the officials of our supposed "*justice system*," who have assisted the **"Great Mormon Conspiracy"**. The Mormons have immorally and diabolically persecuted this man and his family. The duly constituted authorities have illegally and underhandedly assisted in this horrible travesty of justice. Will you, the American public, stand for it without raising a cry of outrage?

You are encouraged to raise a shout to the heavens. Down with public officials who illegally assist any intolerant group to persecute honest men. Down with any corrupt public officials who fail to defend our constitutional rights, 100%. Can we allow them their lofty positions? If so, we deserve the corruption they give us.

Those in legal positions of power who have participated in the evil plot to destroy Bruce Alan Kirschman and his family are:

1. Charles C. Kobayashi, who issued the order granting custody of the Kirschman children to Julie, though California had no jurisdiction and though the children were in their home state of Utah at the time the illegal order was issued.

2. Brett Morgan, the D.A., who filed charges of child abduction and burglary against Kirschman, knowing full well that the charges were

groundless, but determined to shine in **Mormon glory**. It is not known whether Brett Morgan is a Mormon. His actions in this case indicate that he probably is, but if he is only guided by a mean spirit, he has certainly aided the cause of the Mormons who are using our *justice system* so heinously.

3. David Hayes and Richard W. Forbes, Mormons, who traveled with Brett Morgan to El Paso, Texas, to arrest Kirschman **knowing** that the charges against him were **groundless**.

4. Judge Sam Gallan who made it clear in Kirschman's bail hearing in El Paso, that he is uninformed about the law regarding polygamy and that **he** feels that many jurors might find polygamy more distasteful than child molestation. Judge Gallan sees nothing wrong with imposing a 500,000.00 Bail on a man totally innocent of wrong-doing. One must wonder if Judge Gallan is a Mormon? If not, he probably should be. He could find within their ranks, a good many kindred spirits.

About a year and a half ago the above story sort of ended; at least as much of it as the author can relate. After spending nine months in prison, Kirschman was released on a $50,000.00 bond. The author was dissapointed to learn that he jumped bail, fleeing to points unknown. The dissapointment was not for his withdrawing from the evil, corrupted system that had destroyed him and his family; he apparently felt that he could not receive justice. The deck did seem to be stacked against him.

The author believed that at the final hour, in court before a jury of his peers, Kirschman would finally have won the day. He didn't believe he could obtain justice though, and if he did win, he certainly would not in this society, have regained "rights" to help raise his children. Jumping bail was his choice and he has to live with it. He will be a fugitive for many years, if not forever. He and his children are added to the myriad of innocents that our decadent nation has destroyed. Do you think those nine children will love our *justice system*? Not on your tin type!

CHAPTER 5

Let's look further now at our present government, relating its state of being, to the way it should be. The author is qualified, as are you, dear reader, to judge how our government should be functioning. Remember please, that the government of these United States was formed to guarantee our inalienable rights, as specified in the Declaration of Independence. This is what our government should be about.

The Constitution of the USA with its Bill of Rights, does, in its original form, substantially protect our rights. It is of little value though, when our administrators and their henchmen refuse to act within its guidelines. Regulatory agencies, together with the Justice Department and law enforcement organizations, ignore our **Constitutional Rights.** They have become self-perpetuating, self-serving, **Gestapos**.

In this work, the term **Gestapo**, is used frequently to describe agencies similar to the **Gestapo** that operated in Germany during the second world war. That **Gestapo** was a law unto itself. Its members committed atrocities against Jews and Germans alike. Like our many **Gestapos,** they regularly violated with immunity, the rights of the people.

Gestapo, herein, means an organization which exercises wicked, illegal control over our productive citizenry, extracting our resources and imposing ridiculous penalties for our inability to comply with their illegal regulations. These criminal **Gestapos** falsely charge us, the citizens, for failing to comply with their criminal rules. This they do of course, to legally (by lawyer definition) steal from us and to strengthen their strangle-hold on us. The Justice Department, a **Gestapo** and **Gestapo** type law enforcement agencies, assist the other **Gestapos** (agencies) in the illegal oppression of us all.

We, the people, are educated under the auspices of our government. Our local governments raise **from us**, part of the money for our very poor education system. The Federal Government also raises **from us**, monies which it doles back to our schools, with restrictive controls of course.

Our children are taught according to the desires of our wicked government. Along with immorality, they are taught patriotism and that ours is the best system that exists in this world. Our government-controlled schools teach our children falsely that we are a free people. This is no longer true. We are now a nation oppressed by foul criminality, mostly from our own government. We are a nation subjected to many **Gestapos.**

The author has not traveled the world over. Present communication systems though, show us much of the "beingness" of our fellow man in other lands. Many nations now have a higher standard of living than we do. Numerous societies appear to have as much or more freedom than ourselves.

Study of other people's systems, is not the intent of this writing. It should be pointed out though, that we can be easily deceived if we fail to question teachings, simply because we want them to be true.

> Once upon a lovely season
> Our antecedents did have freedom
> It's not that way today
> Our freedom's flown away
> Open your eyes to see the truth
> The light for you will issue forth
> You'll see that in the USA
> Liberty is now passe
> If you ever want to get it back
> You're going to have to leave the pack
> You'll have to stand on your own two feet
> Your courage must be strong and fleet
> If you're a brave and honest person
> Come help us to regain our freedom
> It won't come easily, you know
> For those on top will huff and blow
> They will oppress on every hand
> The people of this once free land
> But if a few will pay the price
> The "right" can merge victorious
> We can o'er throw their evil power
> We can tear down their Eiffel tower
> And oh how happy we will be
> When we've **regained** our **Liberty**

If you are reading this book, you are not without some education. If you have read this far, you're not totally closed-minded. You are not so foolish as to believe that your government can do no wrong, just because you want it to be so. You would have discarded this work before now if you were not somewhat open-minded. The author assumes that you are educated and open-minded and are able to comprehend the following declaration:

Our environment, controlled by nature, is a tremendous recycler. Nature does recycle and restore to natural balance, most of our waste. If we separate and concentrate natural compounds, of course we can make nature's work harder and more time-consuming. For most of our refuse, though, we could not stop nature's recycling process without great effort.

In all things there must be balance. As discussed in Essay 4 of this work, there is a dividing line between good and bad. Temperance, moderation in all things is the healthy rule. Regarding natures recycling of refuse, small quantities of most waste do no harm at all. Large quantities of highly processed and concentrated chemicals can do great harm to nature and to man.

Wisdom tells us to be very careful in seeking the **dividing line** for disposal or treatment of our waste. We may have reached a point wherein some guidelines should be established for control of waste disposal. It is an area that requires **great wisdom** to establish a proper **dividing line**, a proper **balance**. Our government has demonstrated abundantly that almost no wisdom is therein contained.

Our Environmental Protection Agency (EPA) appears to comprise nothing but the typical, bureaucratic buffoons.

> They huff and puff and beat their chest
> They will destroy us all with zest
>
> They'll prosecute with all their might
> And glory in our desperate plight
>
> Don't think they look for justice true
> Their only aim's to bury you
>
> And whether you've done harm or not
> The EPA will take their shot
>
> They are a vile and evil lot
> They are united in the plot
>
> to aid the great conspiracy
> to fight against our **Liberty**

They will take everything you have
You'll go to jail or be their slave

They're shutting down our industry
And oh, how happy they will be

When every knee does bend and bow
And to them perfect fealty show

They will control our every move
Don't you believe it's out of love

They probably don't even know
The reason why they treat us so

To them it's like a drug addiction
To tear and scathe with cool precision

They won't be satiated till
We've nothing left for them to steal

We'll nevermore have **liberty**
While plagued by this foul enemy

The manner in which the evil **Gestapo**, the EPA, is persecuting us, the US citizens, is horrible. They don't prosecute based on harm done. They prosecute rather, based on that which **they** consider to be **potential** for harm. The rules require that we report periodically to the EPA or, similar state **Gestapos**, the status of materials that they consider to be hazardous. Simply failing to file a report can subject one to harassment, fines or worse.

If you store, transport or dispose of materials listed by the EPA as hazardous, you can be fined and imprisoned. Small companies can be fined millions of dollars. Infractors of their evil rules can spend years in prison. Remember that harm to our environment or to mankind is not the criteria for the excessive penalties. The penalties are imposed for failure to bow and scrape to their corrupt regulations and /or to their Lordships, the inquisitioners (agents) of the wicked EPA. Penalties are imposed not for harm done, but rather for the potential for it.

Where is the government that was established strictly and specifically for protection of us, the citizens? Where is the defense of our **liberty**? How can our government create and support these **Gestapos** who usurp diabolically evil and illegal authority over us? Our law enforcement agencies and our justice department (**Gestapos** in their own right), participate 100% with the EPA in bringing down many of our most productive citizens.

The author's own ordeal is insignificant in comparison to most because the jury found him not guilty of EPA charges. Though insignificant, a brief synopsis will be presented because, here is first hand information from which John Q. Public might benefit. For this personal narrative, the author will be called Mr. B; this to shorten and ease dear reader, your efforts in wading through all this.

The trial of Mr. B. began on January 10, 1994, in the Court of Judge Harry Lee Hudspeth. Hudspeth is the presiding Judge of the United States District Court, of the Western District of Texas.

Mr. B. had been arraigned by Magistrate Cole, at which time the five charges were read to him. In an arraignment, possible penalties are explained to the accused before he pleads guilt or innocence. Mr. B. faced the possibility of $2,000,000.00 in fines and ten years in prison.

A few months previous to the Arraignment, a prosecutor named Steve Jurecki, had called Mr. B. to advise him that the government planned to charge him. Jurecki said that though charges weren't serious, as no harm had been done, he (Jurecki) would not like to take unfair advantage of Mr. B. by trying him without representation. Mr. Jurecki suggested that Mr. B. contact Liz Rogers, an attorney with the Public Defenders office. Apparently, Mr. B. didn't appear to possess resources sufficient to fight legal battles against the Federal Government. This was a correct analysis. Mr. B. estimates that the investigation and trial must have cost the tax payers over $500,000.00.. Jurecki, later denied having told Mr. B. that since no harm was done, a prison term would not be sought. It was probably not as serious in his mind as in the victim's. The discussion probably, therefore, was not etched into his memory as it was in the victim's.

As near as he could tell, the investigation by the EPA and the FBI began in 1990. Mr. B. was advised by a friend that the FBI was seeking information about him and the electro-plating operation he'd closed in 1986. Early in '93 a team of EPA, FBI and others, arrived with a search warrant at property in New Mexico, owned by Mr. B.'s brother John. Mr. B. and brother John were away at work. The team began their search however, and they must have been elated at the mountain of what they thought was evidence that they found.

Mr. B. and his brother John have spent their working lives as small business men, contractors in the building industry. They both tried through the years to side-step, or engage in other fields, but always returned to their mainstay, construction. Towards the end of 1978, they both began new enterprises.

John began processing X-ray film and other materials to extract from them, precious metals. Mr. B. set up in the basement of his family home, an electroplating shop. Having a family with small children, would anyone with normal intelligence, bring something dangerous into his home? Of course not. Safety of the chemicals was the first thing checked out before making this move.

Technic Inc. became the first material and equipment supplier for the new venture. Technic is a major supplier in this industry. They have a fine support system to help solve production and technical problems as they arise. In electro plating, tanks are filled with liquids which contain dissolved metals. Each metal can be dissolved by its own chemically compatible materials. Besides the dissolving agents, other chemicals are used to achieve desired results such as speed of deposit, smoothness, brilliance, hardness and ductility.

Supply companies develop plating solutions and most of them aid platers with analysis of the "plating baths". Regular analysis is necessary because the process digests, or uses up the chemicals. Metals for instance, deposit onto the work, or items being plated. Solid metals of the desired type are usually placed in the bath a short distance from the work. These solid metals are called anodes. They dissolve into the bath as the work pieces take metal from it. Anodes don't usually dissolve quite as fast as the work uses the metals. Imbalance can therefore result.

Mr. B. did not become an all-knowing plating expert in the eight years that he operated this, perhaps the worlds smallest, commercial plating operation. He did learn a little, including the fact that plating solutions never need be discarded. As the chemistry changes are detected through analysis, additions are made of materials needed to keep the baths in proper balance. This can be done into infinity.

The EPA lackeys are not refiners or platers or technicians in any of the fields of our industry over which they wield their evil power. They are, rather, mostly college educated bureaucrats. Some are lawyers; many have degrees in business management or related fields. They are not knowledgeable in the fields that they are regulating. The most appropriate, anonymous statement that comes to mind is: "they don't know nothin." They and their henchmen (FBI agents), know as much about how to treat and neutralize cyanide, for example, as lawyers and judges do. Cyanide is a widely used chemical in mining, refining, plating and hardening of metals. Hundreds of thousands of tons of it are used annually, probably millions of tons, world-wide. It can be a deadly poison if used improperly. If mixed with acid, deadly hydrogen cyanide gas is generated. Ingesting cyanide or injecting it into the blood can cause quick death.

People who use cyanide know how to handle it. They don't drink it or chance getting it into their blood stream. Neither do they mix it with acid. Back in the early 80's, there was an incident in Michigan, wherein, a man was killed in a refining operation that used large quantities of cyanide. Surely there must have been other cases. They have been few enough though, that the author has never heard of one, have you? Of course, intentional misuse has been reported (the Jim Jones incident), and cyanide has been used in executions. The intent here though is to look at the industrial use of chemicals.

EPA agents act as though cyanide will kill off whole cities, if industrialists are allowed to exercise educated discretion in its use. These simpletons (EPA agents) would have us all peeing our pants in fear of the terrible industrialists who use cyanide or other chemicals, not understood by them (EPA simpletons). Most compounds of cyanide with other elements are relatively harmless. Free cyanide is the feared culprit. It is easily neutralized with the chlorine that many of you use to fight bacteria in your swimming pools. Another very effective neutralizer of free cyanide is sunlight.

Cyanide is,of course, just one of many chemicals that can be dangerous if misused. It can be very deadly, yet substances and mechanisms used commonly by us all do thousands of times more damage. Should we outlaw the use of automobiles because people are killed by them? Should we stop using natural gas and electricity? Every day many of us suffer or die from accidents with these utilities. Once in a very long while, industrial chemicals are culprits in accidents. Your very real and powerful enemy, the **Gestapo**,called the EPA, exerts great energy in frightening us, the public. They spend our resources to frighten us and to subjugate and close down our industry. Don't be fooled into thinking their costly regulations help to create a safer or cleaner environment. Industry knows far better than they how to operate efficeintly and safely.

Attempted compliance with EPA B.S. drives the bad guys underground, turns some good guys bad, and puts many productive entrepreneurs out of business. It also raises considerably the price that we all must pay for products that we need and use every day.

Asbestos warrants brief discussion. It probably caused some medical problems for workmen in the mines and manufacturing centers that processed it. It is a classic example though, of badly misplacing the **dividing line** between government interference and proper, responsible control by industry. When truly acting as our protector, the government has a right to penalize any and all, in or out of industry, who do **intentional harm**. Of course, if the **line** is properly positioned, penalties will be commensurate with, or in proportion to, the amount of harm done.

Some medical researchers opined that asbestos might cause cancer. Government fear-mongers jumped on the idea and quickly crushed a major industry. The author worked in and around asbestos for many years. The industry he worked in was large, employing many thousands who inhaled fine particles of asbestos. The author has never heard of lung problems for workers in this industry, nor has he experienced any. The author believes the asbestos **scare** to be just that.

Without real proof of harm done, our government killed the multi-billion Dollar productive asbestos industry at the expense of private industry and of the thousands who worked therein. They created in its stead, a multi billion dollar destructive industry at the expense of the American people. For many years now, it has been required that every public building in this country that is remodeled or demolished has to first undergo removal of asbestos bearing products. Many wonderful floor coverings, roofing, insulating and other building materials used to contain, and be better for, asbestos. Asbestos removal is tightly regulated by EPA flunkies. Because infractions of their stupid, excessively stringent and corrupt regulations is very costly. The gamblers who enter the removal industry must charge accordingly. The cost to the American public is tremendous. The initial fear campaign succeeded though, and this slave society has swallowed the B.S. We continue to dig deeper to pay for the opportunity afforded by Uncle for us to **bend over**.

Crude, rough language is not considered by the author to be conducive to clean, clear thinking. It is generally poor taste to use the baser forms of expression but, a little color is sometimes needed and may help to appropriately and accurately aid in recognition of truth. A friend of the author and a brilliant, well educated, very refined and talented man, expressed very aptly, the most appropriate term that can be applied to the lackeys of our **Gestapos**. Mr. R. Gordon's term for them is, "Butt Pirates."

Brother John had allowed a bankrupted contractor and business associate to store some construction equipment and materials on his (Johns) property in Anthony, New Mexico. Included with the equipment were approximately 200 empty, 50/gallon steel drums. These had been used as bases for platforms upon which small portable houses had been built. The search team in their wisdom concluded that these 200 drums (Approx.) which had been emptied of construction adhesives some twenty years previous, must have contained hazardous waste. They decided further that Mr. B must have illegally dumped them somewhere in the desert.

About mid 1986, Mr. B closed his plating shop, selling most of it, but keeping for possible future use or sale, about thirty, fifty gallon drums of plating solutions. Some were useable and some needed chemical adjustment for efficient use. At any rate, none of Mr. B's materials were waste or hazardous.

A very wise man said: *A little knowledge is a dangerous thing. Drink deep or taste not at all*. In the spirit of this wisdom, some background to Mr. B's ordeal will herein be presented. This, to demonstrate how misunderstandings can take place and how unscrupulous and cowardly individuals can aid and abet our vile **Gestapos** in persecution of us all. Those who saw the lying and enhanced news stories about Mr. B. should be given something to look at from his side of the equation.

The *huge* plating shop was moved in 1980. Mr. B and his brother John merged the plating and refining operations into a leased building on Paisano Drive in West El Paso. In 83, the businesses separated again; John moved his refining back to his place in Anthony, New Mexico.

An important factor in this story is the Magnum Corporation. They "sub let" a portion of the building from late 1984 into early 1986. Magnum set up a laboratory to analyze ore and to develop methods for extraction of precious metals therefrom. Magnum's man, Cezar Fulton, a mining engineer, brought materials from Mexico and elsewhere for analysis and experimentation. They used a wide variety of chemicals in working with various raw materials. Magnum Mining dissolved early in 1986.

In 1986, Mr. B. sold his shop to an enterprise headed by Don Littlepage. Littlepage "sub let" a portion of the lower floor of the building leased by Mr. B on Paisano Drive. Littlepage operated on a larger scale than had Mr. B. and worked with other processes. He plated some materials that used small amounts of components that are on the EPA list of hazardous materials. Mr. B. was unaware of this at the time. Littlepage stayed only about a year. He moved his shop to Juarez, Mexico. He said that he would not subject himself to the meddling of the EPA. In this he showed wisdom.

Mr. B. continued to lease the building, using it primarily for storage of construction materials, tools and such. The construction business which Mr. B. had returned to, was operated mainly at construction sites and from a home office. The building on Paisano was therefore visited seldom. A man named Ben Hladky, lived on the upper floor and "sort of" watched over the place.

During the time between 1986 and 1989, Mr. B used the building just for storage of plating materials which he expected to someday use or sale. During this time frame, on a rare visit, Mr. B. discovered Cezar Fulton using the building. Fulton was working with an investor and was experimenting with ore concentrates brought from Mexico. His story was that the concentrates had good metal values that needed a practical method of extraction. He was trying to develop a method in Mr. B.'s building with Mr. B.'s equipment and utilities. Cezar volunteered to pay rent, which, of course, never materialized. He told Mr. B. that he was using sulfuric acid in his experimental process. This didn't work. He then tried a cyanide process. Mr. B. observed drums of sodium cyanide in the area being used by Fulton.

In 1985, representatives of the Texas Water Commission (TWC) began calling on Mr. B. The TWC is a sort of surrogate of, or a Jr. EPA. They act at least as though they had shared a common womb. Toadies for these **Gestapos** have the "God Syndrome." They are, in their minds, all knowing, all powerful, elitist masters, of us, the lower life forms, who waste our lives in the drudgery of producing the needs of the human family.

If you have not as yet deduced the character of Mr. B., listen up. Whatever else he may, or may not be, Mr. B is not so cowardly that he'll allow bureaucratic boobs, "Butt Pirates," sodomites, to diddle around in, and control his business. The author probably knows every filthy word and expression in English and Spanish and a good many in German. The author is totally at a loss though, for words to adequately describe the lunacy of a government that will rape, rob, sodomize, interfere with and will control, negatively, its main supporters, as does ours.

> Can anyone possibly describe, in depth, our tale of woe?
> Is there any possibility that meager words can show
> The great extent of evil, to which our government will go?
> No! Mere words fail, they're weak and pale
> They lack the power you know
> To truly show the heartlessness, that shakes us to and fro
> And puts to shame the poet, who prays the words will flow
> But cannot find the proper phrase in heaven or below

The plating shop of Mr. B was tiny, occupying during most of its existence, about 500 Sq. Ft.of a12,000 Sq. Ft. building. The building was filled up though, with remnants of brother John's refinery and Magnum Mining Corp.'s laboratory and leavings. Mr. B also had in the building, a small machine shop, along with tools and equipment for use in construction work.

John's refining operation recovered silver from X-ray film. Most of the film was stored in empty 50 gallon, cardboard drums. During the time that the TWC was harassing Mr B. there were approximately 200 of these barrels throughout the building.   Though John had moved his operation to New Mexico, he continued to store some materials in the building, off and on, as it was convenient to most of his "pick up points" in El Paso. Mr. B. also used empty cardboard barrels to store various materials such as, tumbling media (corn husks), and a variety of items purchased at auctions for re-sale.

Imagine the glee of the TWC agents who discovered the Plater (feared user of chemicals) that had hundreds of barrels strewn around. Here was a chance for exercise of their great power over a hated industrialist. Mr. B.'s operation was much too small to qualify, but gave the appearance to the unknowing, of being much grander in scale than it was.

Jim Goris, **gestapo** agent extraordinaire for the TWC, called on Mr. B. several times, always reminding him that his (Goris') power was great and that Mr. B. had better comply with regulations. Mr. B is no genius, nor is he well educated. Neither is he without God-given intelligence. He knew of a certainty that, as he did not use hazardous materials, these b...stards had no legitimate authority over him. What he could not be sure of though, was how much evil could be brought to bear, by way of harassment, by these emissaries of Satan.

A neighbor in the complex processed chili. This neighbor had a swimming pool atop his building. The pool ruptured, draining through his building, across the roadway, along Mr. B.'s building and pooled at a corner thereof. The pool had a greenish tint to it, which could have come from the chilies or from a variety of materials. Goris demanded of Mr. B., a cleanup, to include soil removal and laboratory analysis of the material. Chrome was suspected, which can be a hazardous material.

No! Mr. B is not by nature, subservient. No, Mr. B did not believe in Goris' greatness, nor the legality or rightness of his demands. He did believe though, the threat that if he failed to comply, Goris would bring in a state cleanup team and that per Goris' threat, it could cost Mr. B, 250,000.00 to 5000,000.00. It doesn't take a genius to know that a little guy, barely eking out a living for his family, has not the ability to fight the government. They have the power to take from us, the resources with which to fight us. What a *glorious condition*, words cannot describe it.

Mr. B. spent a few thousand, hard earned dollars in cleaning up the neighbor's mess and filling the low spot with concrete to avoid further pooling from accidents or from rain. Lab analysis of the soil showed suspected chrome to be at the same levels as the surrounding area contained. Just the amount that nature had distributed throughout that part of Texas.

Knowing that he couldn't win in fights against the monster, Mr. B gave up the plating business. This was no great loss to our society. The business never employed more than five or six people anyway. It was not very profitable. The TWC cannot be blamed entirely for destroying this tiny enterprise. They were simply the added problem that was unacceptable and helped to make up Mr. B.'s mind. He might have fought them on level ground. There wasn't any.

Mr. B. went back to contracting in mid 1986. He was grossly under-capitalized. Littlepage had bought the plating shop with a note and payments that would help a little with support of the family till the new venture could begin to pay.

At the end of 1986, Mr. B. completed a contract at Ft. Bliss, Texas, and received $700,000.00 from work that cost $1,100,000.00. Mr. B. was, at this time, instructed by his Landlord, Don Studdard, Attorney, to remove all plating materials from the building on Paisano Drive. Studdard had also been harassed by the TWC.

Financially, Mr. B. was not in wonderful shape. Five dependent children and a wife, precluded any thought of p...sing off any hard earned-resources. Simply dumping his non-hazardous, valuable, useable or saleable materials, never crossed his mind. He moved and caused to have moved, his materials to other properties that he was using.

A relationship to a key player in this scenario should be mentioned. Mr. Darrel Esslinger played a huge part in events that took over Mr. B.'s life, bringing the EPA with their cohorts, the FBI, swooping down upon him. Mr. B., feels that he gave Esslinger friendship and help. Apparently, Esslinger did not feel the friendship nor recognize the help as such; but yes, Mr. B. provided contracual work for him at greater than necessary cost. Mr. B. further gave Esslinger work that he could have done himself to save expense. These things were done out of friendship and because Esslinger needed to provide for his family.

A history surrounding the **Esslinger, Mr. B. relationship**, was originally described here. It has been deleted because it is quite personal and not in keeping with the spirit of this book. Brothers John and Joseph suggested that the Esslinger story leaves the impression that the author is bitter and that this could be construed as a partial motivator for this effort. The author has searched his soul and does not believe he is bitter, nor motivated in the least by personal attacks by any person or agency. Personal happenings have, of course, helped to mold his character and his beliefs, which direct his actions.

This personal story is presented, not by way of complaint for personal harrassment, but as earlier stated, because it is typical of similar happenings throughout our nation. This history is presented in the hope that you, dear reader, will hear and fear and act to attempt to save some of your poor abused, falsely accused, fellow men.

You must understand that no man deserves **God's gift of freedom**, unless he is willing to defend the rights of his peers to the same **freedom**. We sit by, allowing or even helping our evil *justice sysem* to persecute good men with "nit picky" laws which are ridiculous to a point of corruption. Every time we allow an innocent person to be mistreated by our *justice system*, the **freedom** of us all is diminished.

The **Esslinger, Mr. B. story** does somewhat depict the kind of people who are coming forth from our breediong ground. In other words, persons are being produced in our environment with tendencies like those described in this depiction. Because the story may not be harmonious with the intent of this story, much of this part of this story has been deleted, leaving only the author's claim that Esslinger did him considerable harm before instigating the EPA investigation.

With or without more information about Esslinger, you can probably understand the following natural phenomenon. The human being feels great need to justify actions, at least to himself or herself. If you damage someone, you must somehow rationalize some justification. You must decide somehow that the damaged party deserved what you dished out. It is a rare person indeed that can damage another without developing hatred for that recipient of unfair actions.

Darrel Esslinger cheated and hurt Mr. B. after having been helped by him. Darrel had to develop hatred. In this case the hatred had to be acted upon. Mr.

Esslinger moved materials for Mr. B from El Paso, Texas to Anthony, New Mexico. He moved without Mr. B's knowledge, some materials left behind at the El Paso site by Don Littlepage and Cezar Fulton.

The EPA flunkies must have been elated when Darrell called to tell them he may have transported hazardous materials for Mr. B. Imagine their joy when after brief investigation, they saw a chance to set legal precedence with an individual. It was the first case of its kind in the Western District of Texas and in Southern New Mexico. Their teeth had been sharpened somewhat on corporations, but they have as yet, less than desired power over individuals.

Yes! They must have been pleased at the opportunity to prosecute this seemingly defenseless ninny, this poor white trash.

> Oh how they gloat and glory
> While they punish us, the lowly
> Had we the serfs, done proper homage
> They could not show to us their plumage
> And so when we, the wretched fools
> Fail to learn and keep their rules
> They laugh and revel in the sport
> And catch us where the hair is short
> To batter us makes them feel grand
> It justifies their evil stand
> They think it elevates their throne
> To beat us down and lay us prone

Well they went after Mr. B. with zeal and gusto and seemingly, with joyous pleasure.

Steve Jurecki, a Federal Prosecutor in El Paso, called to suggest that Mr. B talk to Miss Rogers at the public defender's office. Jurecki stated that he would feel an unfair imbalance in prosecuting one like Mr. B. who had no legal background. He also stated plainly that the charges were not so serious as to warrant imprisonment, as apparently no harm had been done. This, of course, was true. No harm had been done by Mr. B. through any act, knowingly or otherwise, that could be laid at the door of his defunct plating operation. Here, another truth must be spelled out:

Freedom does not exist when government or corrupt officials enact corrupt laws which castigate citizens for acts that are thought by the "Godless" to have potential for harm. Righteous law establishes <u>freedom</u>

and <u>defends</u> liberty. **Righteous law protects the innocent (law abiding) from the sinner (law breaker) for the express purpose of maintaining <u>liberty</u> for those who earn it. Extremely heavy penalties are prescribed today by our "Godless" government, through its <u>Gestapos</u>, for acts that <u>they say</u> have <u>potential for harm.</u> This is <u>corruption.</u>**

The following parable is just that, a similitude of regular happenings throughout our land.

A chicken farmer, named Joe, operating at the west side of a reservoir, found that government regulations increased his costs beyond reason. If he raised his prices to profitable levels, his clientele couldn't afford to buy eggs or chicken. He decided that his family deserved to have him put his efforts into more lucrative endeavors.

He put his business up for sale. The chicken coop was leased, but he owned roosts, incubators, lighting, heating and cooling equipment, egg and meat processing equipment, and of course, trucks, barrels and shovels with which to handle the chicken manure. The beginning of Joe's economic demise it seems was a saturation of the manure market.

Manufactured, chemical fertilizers, have gradually become more popular of course, to the detriment of the more odoriferous manure. Chicken farms at best are highly competitive. The manure sales can be the difference between profit and loss.

Joe lost a "sub lease" tenant. The landlord introduced him to another potential renter. Resources were consumed in rearranging and preparing a portion of the leased building for the new tenant. A rental agreement had been reached which would include payment to Joe for his expenses in improving and managing the building. The landlord who brought to Joe the renter, was not sole owner of the property. His partner decided, to hell with that, not wanting Joe to have income from the improvements and ignoring his partners magnanimous efforts, he told the tenant she could bypass Joe and rent directly from himself.

When the new tenant had no further need for Joe's goodwill, she demanded that he remove some stored barrels of chicken manure from a basement area beneath her portion of the building. This storage area had been reserved out by Joe, but he lost control and was required by the landlord to do her bidding and kiss her foot... The lawyer, partner, really didn't want Joe in his building with his financial problems and his stinking chicken manure. Joe had to walk lightly to avoid further problems.

Excretion from chickens contains ammonia. When really ripe and heated, the scent is **not** that of roses. To move the barrels from storage they had to be opened and transferred by pumping. Weather was cool, the scent was weak, but not nonexistent. Jane was, as you might expect, a highly refined and cultivated young woman. She was the type that would probably faint with mortification if her date slipped up in public by breaking wind with a small squeaker.

When the sweet scent embraced her sensitive nasal passages, Jane lost her sense of reality. She decided it might cause Cancer, Aids or some such. She called in the "powers that be" to investigate this horrible potential for debilitating or life threatening happenstance. The "powers that be", the agency for investigation of natural fertilizers, agreed with Jane that these odors could be dangerous. They required that the landlord acquire laboratory analysis of a manure stain found at a loading dock area.

The landlord complied with instructions, obtaining a lab determination. The official opinion was that a million tons of this material, if dumped into the reservoir, might cause temporary indigestion for those who might drink the water. It could also leave a slight pungency on the persons of skinny dippers. The few milligrams though, that constituted the stain on the dock, could not be determined to be of sufficient quantity to cause discomfort.

The manure regulators were dismayed. They were unable at that time to justify further, shitty harassment. They went on to vex other inferior life forms and to bide their time for, *well they knew, the silly fly* (Joe) *would soon be back again.* Time went by and *various agonies did intervene.* The time came when the landlord told Joe to remove from the premises, all stored chicken manure. It was all removed to a location at the north end of the reservoir, to the yard of Joe's friend.

It turned out that Jane had a friend living close to the chicken hotel who noticed the moving of the dreaded manure and notified the regulators. They decided to try again for fame, by inflicting pain on Joe. They charged him with hauling his stinking shit on a road that was on a levy along side the reservoir. The logic they tried to sell to the Jury, was that Joe created potential for great harm to the public. He might have gotten into a rush to catch the Cowboys versus the Forty-Niners in the play-offs. He might have driven too fast on the levy and rolled over, dumping all twenty barrels into the drink. Another real possibility was that a tire might have blown out on the left side (reservoir side) of the truck. This could very possibly have pulled the truck into the water.

If the sealed drums had ended up in the lake and if the irresponsible Joe had been killed so that he couldn't retrieve them, with time, the drums might have ruptured. Had this scenario unfolded, about one part of manure per ten billion parts of water could have resulted. Think about it. If the sun and other natural recycling processes such as plant life didn't get it, that one part per billion might have ended up in the milk of some cow, or worse.

Joe should have been convicted. The prosecutors in selecting the Jury excused people who admitted that they ate eggs or chicken. Also dismissed were any who ate organically grown vegetables, or drank non-pasteurized milk. Yes! They should have won. Everyone knows that the manure regulators won't bring charges that are not true. It was proved in the trial though, that the old Studebaker truck had a governor on the engine. It wouldn't go faster than 30 MPH. Also, tires were proven to be mostly new. One was slightly worn, but it was on the right side of the truck, away from the water. The defense attorney convinced the Jury that a blowout would have pulled the truck away from the water. In short, Joe was found not guilty. He escaped the life imprisonment and the 2,000,000.00 Fine, sought by the regulators.

The news media of course, had portrayed Joe all over the southwest as a terrible, shitty guy. His family, being human, were much embarrassed by this. Some people though don't watch the lying news stories. Joe is still able to eke out a meager living at his new venture. He now sells charcoal breathing masks, which filter out and cushion bad odors.

The parable about Joe, though, slightly exaggerated, does truly depict the attitudes and actions of our **"Godless Gestapos."** Throughout our nation, hard working men and women are harassed on the whims of idiots. Further, in large numbers, productive citizens are jailed and otherwise penalized, by our own government. Have we totally lost our senses, that we will tolerate such cannibalism? Our government is truly eating its own leg and is unable to see where its indigestion comes from.

An important angle on this case was a relationship between Mr. B. and Technic Incorporated. Technic Inc., like other plating suppliers, employs trained technicians to assist platers with technical problems. Another service Technic offers is refining of precious metals, which over time, develop as residues from plating with these metals.

Mr. B. struck a bargain with Technic. They agreed to supply a new gold bath in exchange for gold which Mr. B. was to refine under their direction. The deal was that they would analyze the residues and recommend the refining method. Mr. B. sent material for Technic's analysis. Technic sent the gold bath. Technic never supplied the promised refining method.

With brother John's help, a 12 Oz., 98% pure bar of gold was finally refined and sent to Technic. Had Technic kept the agreement to recommend a refining method, the gold should have reached them when it had a value of about $8,000.00. Working out a method was slow. Gold prices were greatly reduced by delivery time.

Small refineries often cheat on purity analysis, but in this case it was ridiculous. Technic gave credit for approximately three ounces of gold. John had developed a reputation as an accurate assayer. Mr. B. refused to take the shafting from Technic. He took steps to protect himself legally from them..

The prosecutors later put a Technic representative on the witness stand. He told the Jury that plating solutions have a short useable life. His estimate was about three years. This young man did not simply misunderstand the use of plating solutions. He was not greatly knowledgeable, but he knew very well that he was lying to the court. No one can work in his capacity and not know that plating baths have as long a life as proprietors want to give them. The attempt was to prove that solutions stored by Mr. B were really waste and maybe even hazardous. The charges were for storing, transporting and disposing of hazardous waste in Texas. Two counts were charged in New Mexico, storing and disposing of waste. In all, five charges were filed, each with possibility of two years imprisonment. Ten years was potentially possible, together with 2,000,000.00 in fines.

During the arraignment, Magistrate Cole remarked that due to the Chapter 13 case (Re-organizational bankruptcy), the government couldn't expect to collect more than a 100.00 or so per month. Cole joked that it would take into the year 3000 plus, for Mr. B.. to pay this fine. The court laughed and so did Mr. B., but he couldn't help reflecting that this was a very real possibility.

The public defender's office juggled the case till it fell into the hands of Marc Robert (pronounced Robair). Mr. B is strong willed or maybe more appropriately, opinionated and obstinate. People of his ilk usually term each other as "one way" or "bull headed." You get the picture. Marc Robert had a difficult time and must have considered withdrawing in the early stages of preparation. As time went on though, he and the defendant learned to feel better about one another.

Mr. Robert showed himself to be a rare bird among his contemporaries in law. He demonstrated genuine concern. He turned out to be a man of compassion, a humanist and he finally seemed to believe in the defendant's innocence. Robert sent off for EPA regulations which he doggedly studied. It is extremely complicated material. With years of study, most of us couldn't fully understand these regulations. Robert is very capable, took the time, studied hard and prepared a sound defense, thank **God!**

Before accepting help from the public defender's office, Mr. B had sought, or at least investigated, the possibility of hiring an attorney. The requirement of years of indebtedness was not the deterrent. It was the unwillingness of the lawyers to consider the case without an absolute guarantee, of an outrageous fee.

Public defenders are paid a salary—win, lose, or draw, they fare the same. One is fortunate indeed, to find a public defender who is both capable and will put his heart into one's case. Mr. B. was extremely fortunate and will be eternally grateful to Marc Robert. He is not among the majority of his peers who are aptly and correctly described in this work. He is the one in a couple of hundred, that is a decent human being. Presently, he is in private practice in Albuquerque. If he fares well, it will be due to his brilliance and his willingness to work hard. If he does not get rich, it will be due to his compassion in a world of greedy and unethical wolves. The author prays for him.

When faced with danger and misery, many of us turn to God. Faced with years of imprisonment, and then life long poverty, Mr. B. became more prayerful and more studious of the scriptures. In the Old Testament, in the book of Isaiah, he read verse 7 of the 50th chapter, which state the following: *If God's Law is truly written in your heart, you need not fear the reproach of men.* The words of Isaiah are great pertaining to the last days. Isaiah, chapter 2 verse 2 tells us he speaks of the last days. Read the entire second chapter if you want to see a perfect description, in language of old, of our country in its present state of being. This chapter also describes some of what we're faced with in the near future.

Mr. B had to stop and reflect upon himself and his attitudes. He had to admit that he is but a man and is subject to the temptations of the flesh. He has the weaknesses typical of mankind. Another thing that Mr. B. had to admit to himself is that he loves the idea of Liberty. He loves the **"law of God"** with all his heart. Mr. B. hates very passionately the destruction of our freedoms. He is appalled at observances on every hand, of his fellows infringing, knowingly, on each other's rights. No! Mr. B is not always able to do all that he wants to do. Yes, he has failed at times to comply fully with obligations or duties, though, never out of choice. **"God's law"** is truly in his heart.

Mr. B had to admit to himself that nothing in this life, is to him, more important than **"GODS PERFECT LAW OF LIBERTY"**, freedom for himself, his family and his countrymen. Admitting this, Mr. B had to know that he need not fear his enemies. In this case, the **Lord God** was duty bound by his own word, to help.

A great load was lifted from his shoulders. He did not have perfect knowledge, but was strongly impressed that he would prevail in the upcoming ordeal. He does believe **God** to be truthful. He believed that he would be a recipient of **God's** promise through Isaiah.

The prosecutor, with the mighty government behind him, wove a tale of horror. He showed some pictures of many awful looking, deteriorating cardboard barrels of harmless materials. Many of these were ores or concentrates being processed by John. They looked ugly, but were nonhazardous, harmless, natural elements. Of course, Mr. B being a terrible person, should be punished by whatever means possible. So what if the awful looking stuff wasn't his? Doesn't the *end justify the means*?

One evening during the trial, El Paso Channels 7 and 9 showed to all the southwest, pictures of John's property. Thereat were John's materials, harmless, but ugly, Mr. B's materials and materials belonging to Littlepage and Fulton. These lovely purveyors of *truth* were not satisfied with simply showing and lying about what was there. They also edited into their film, an awful looking caldron of an orangish yellow, fuming, frothing, sizzling material, unrecognizable to John or Mr. B. Anyone seeing the awful mess would be hard pressed to doubt the news story of environmental rape. In fairness, Judge Hudspeth asked the Jurors to disqualify themselves if they'd seen and been swayed by this story.

Shortly before the trial started, a reporter from channel 4 news asked John for an interview. He agreed, with the stipulation that his words would not be changed or twisted. Asked if his brother had transported and deposited the hazardous materials, he answered, "yes, he brought them here, but they are not hazardous." Which five words do you think the purveyors of truth cut out of the recording? The television program showed the lying reporter asking John if his brother had transported and deposited the hazardous materials. John was then shown to give for answer, a simple, yes. Oh yes, we can take great pride in our wonderful news media. Yes our Constitution guarantees freedom of speech. Libelous lies, which can damage reputations, were never intended to have constitutional protection. The American people deserve better. Justices who will uphold this sort of injustice are corrupt and evil. They should be dismissed and severely punished.

For acids to be considered hazardous, they must measure 2 or below on a <u>PH scale.</u> This is simply a measuring scale which determines causticity and acidity, down to a level of 0. Above 2 is alright. Below 2, inclusive is considered corrosive. Certain barrels were on property adjacent to John's. Mr. B. had an option to purchase this land and had a right to use it. Some of these barrels had been opened, either by trespassing snoops or by investigating, **Gestapo** henchmen. Almost a year before the trial, Mr. B. requested through his attorney, permission from the FBI to move the barrels. The desire was to consolidate, adjust, cover and protect the materials. Of course, safety to vandals was also a consideration. The FBI said, "absolutely not". To touch these barrels would be tampering with evidence.

The barrels on the adjacent property that had a tendency towards corrosivity, were plating baths with a sulfuric acid component. Water with a PH of 7 will evaporate, lowering the PH of acid containing solutions.

The government witness, a chemist testified that these barrels had a PH of about 2, which is corrosive. The defendant in rebuttal, explained that simple evaporation would have lowered the PH and that simple addition of water, not allowed by the FBI, would have raised the PH, back to above corrosive levels. Of course, these were terribly *dangerous chemicals* that they wouldn't allow Mr. B to adjust or move to a safer place. Of course, he should be in jail for possessing such *dangerous chemicals* that the FBI felt were alright to leave exposed to trespassers.

After testimony explained the evaporating and adding back of water technique for lowering and raising PH, the prosecutor did a re-cross of his witness. The brilliant chemist explained to the jury how hydrochloric acid will break down and dissipate along with evaporating water. This, of course, shot down Mr. B.'s explanation of why the PH was lower than when materials had been stored.

The prosecutor probably didn't know the difference between acids, nor did he think the Jury would know the difference, nor did he care. Mr. B and the brilliant chemist both knew the materials in question contained sulfuric acid. Yes HCL will break down and dissipate, almost as fast as water. Adding water back though, will still raise the PH accordingly. The chemist was enlisted to help the prosecutor. He knew which lies would be undetected or would be confusing to the Jury. It was never known, whether the Jury understood that the baths were based in sulfuric acid, not hydrochloric.

The star witness for the prosecution, the young representative from Technic Inc. told his lies about the short life span of plating baths. The two prospective jurors who may have had experience with plating shops, had of course, been dismissed by the prosecutor. They would have helped fellow jurors to see the pergury of this witness, the Technic Inc. employee.

The promise in Isaiah proved up. Witnesses for the defense spoke clearly, truthfully with authority and with the might of right.

Ray Molina, shop superintendent and share holder in El Paso Plating Works for many years, testified clearly and concisely. Among other things he testified that Technic's man was inept, inexperienced, and generally didn't know what he was talking about. Mr. Bill Greuling Jr., President of El Paso Plating Works, also testified as to the Technic man's ineptness and told of baths in their shop that were 35 or so years old and still working well. This biased witness though, did not testify simply from inexperience. He flat out lied. Of course, one *would never suspect, would one*, that the problems between Technic and Mr.B could possibly have influenced his willingness to lie for the prosecution? It is not expected to surprise you, dear reader, that the government would allow such testimony.

These men, Molina and Greuling, witnesses for Mr. B, were facing their own similar problems. They were well aware that standing up in defense of truth would anger their enemies and strengthen their resolve. These men of honor and courage stepped forward and did their duty. Mr. B is in their debt. He feels terrible for them. They did not fare so well as did He.

Robert Simon, a genius and a chemist, had helped Mr. B. immeasurably to learn and operate his small plating business. Mr Simon was totally familiar with the operation and therefore able to testify to the nonehazardous nature of materials used therein. He was also a good character witness.

Brother John has a keen, quick mind. He speaks from the heart and would not compromise his principles with anything but truth. He took credit for ownership of some of the awful looking materials the EPA lackeys were attempting to lay at Mr. B.'s door.

Norm Reber, an old friend, a brilliant and highly educated industrialist, had spent some time in Mr. B.'s shop. Reber has a photographic memory. He also has that "need to know" trait that causes him to pay close attention to details in all situations. He knew that Mr. B used nonhazardous materials exclusively and he so testified. Reber was also a very good character witness.

Even Mr. B.'s wife Joy testified to her belief in his honesty. Although juries expect wives to be on the side of their husbands, she generated sincerity. She was a good witness. It is hard to beat the forthrightness of an honest and guileless person.

A jury must listen to opposing witnesses and must decide who is telling the truth. In this case, the jury probably knew very little about the materials and the chemistry involved. It must have been a difficult task. The witnesses for the defense, were to a man and woman, impressive in their demeanor. They all did exude integrity and honesty. They were clear, concise, straight forward. Persons of honor came to Mr. B.'s defense and confounded the enemy.

What a contrast these men were to the few who could have helped, but were frightened out of their wits. Littlepage for example, used a chrome bearing immersion bath to fix a zinc finish. This operation was performed in the building where Littlepage left much refuse and materials; the building he had sub-leased from Mr. B. for about a year. Maybe he was just frightened, or maybe he had to hate Mr. B. because his son had stolen from him (Mr. B.) and Littlepage knew and allowed it. At any rate, Littlepage lied, claiming never to have used chrome in the building.

Cezar Fulton, when asked about his cyanide, denied having used or left it. He claimed to have tried to use soap in his experiments. Mr. Robert decided not to call these wondrous men as witnesses. The court room would probably have resonated to their quaking.

No! the author is not trying to make enemies. He knows though, that these men already must hate him to justify their actions. Neither is he at all concerned about the opinion of cowards and liars.

Another man, Travis Hausler, a dentist in El Paso, had caused some drums of oil to be sent to John's yard in Anthony. When asked to take credit for this, he said, "of course." He offered to testify if needed. He was not needed, but it is always gratifying to find men of honor and courage. Gratitude and respect go to Hausler.

Mr. B. is deeply grateful to the rare and fine attorney, Marc Robert. He is profoundly grateful to his stalwart witnesses. He'll be forever grateful to the jury who wrestled with the very complicated information. They couldn't help but feel that the government wouldn't press charges without justification. They were not willing to convict though, without proof positive. Had they been less dedicated to right, this would have been written from behind bars. How sweet were the words, "not guilty", to all five charges. The news media did carry the words of a law enforcement officer, who said: *He got out of this, but we'll get him for something.*

Imagine the author's chagrin, when a good man, who had helped him was convicted on similar charges. Bill Greuling Jr. and Ray Molina were both tried for infractions of the EPA **Gestapo's** vilely evil code. One was found guilty. The other became convinced of the futility of fighting against a stacked deck and accepted a "plea-bargain."

This book would have been ready for publishing some two years ago, but for the horror story of the Greuling family and the destruction of their family business in El Paso, Texas. They owned the El Paso Plating Works. The author tried hard to convince Bill Greuling J., who was President of that firm to write his story for inclusion in this writing. Mr.Greuling was tried less than one year after he testified for the author, helping to exonerate him (the author). Mr. Greuling didn't fare so well. He was convicted and sentenced to two years in prison, which time he is presently serving at the Biggs Field Federal Prison.

Mr. Greuling put off writing his story, as he and his attorney felt that publication of the same might prejudice his chance for a succesful appeal. After the appeal failed to give him a new trial or reverse the decision, it is assumed that he would fear that publishing the truth about the underhanded and evil proceedings could adversely affect his chances for an early hoped for parole. If he should be parolled, one must believe he would still hold his peace, as he would fear parole cancellation on one pretext or another if he were to speak out. In conversations with Mr. Greuling, the author was given tidbits of information, which he will herein pass on.

The reader should understand that this brief story of Greuling's rail-roading is heresay. It is not written by Bill Greuling, nor has Bill been asked for permission to publish it. The author feels that Mr. Greuling would be jeopardizing himself to give permission and feels at the same time that the public should know something about the case. This is very short, because information simply cannot be aquired beyond the few remarks that slipped from Greuling during the times that the author tried unsuccesfuly to get him to write or tell his story for publication. It is hoped that the time will come that he can feel free to tell all without fear of reprisals by his government against himself and his family.

111

The author began a small electro-plating business in 1978. For years he hounded El Paso Plating administrators for needed information about the business he was trying to learn. They were always helpful and often cautioned the author about safety precautions that should be excercised relative to care of chemicals that could possibly be construed as dangerous or hazardous. This is not heresay or conjecture. The author has perfect knowlege of the intent of the Greulings and their supervisory help to maintain a clean and safe environment.

EPA regulations have been developing ever since the inception of this diabolical **Gestapo**. Every year new regulations are added and new laws come into being as these enemies of humanity acquire more law through precedence. The EPA administrators themselves and their lawyer henchmen cannot possibly understand all that their vast books contain. Be that as it may, they target certain industries, including the plating industry in order to gain strength by having regulations become laws through precedence, thereby giving their *glorious honors* more and more power over their fellow men, particularly over those who are producing the wealth of our nation from which these EPA agents and their helpers are paid.

During the trial of the author, he was told that the FBI was after the Greulings. Bill told the author that in taking his wife to dinner he often saw certain FBI agents following and watching them, sometimes through field glasses. Yes, the Greulings knew they were under attack. They thought, though, that they were complying with law, and they couldn't conceive of the underhanded methods and the outright dishonesty the government will go to get convictions.

The government managed to frighten Ray Molina, a shareholder and production Superintendent, into a plea bargain. He then, with immunity, testified against Greuling. The author can't say one way or the other about the veracity of Ray's testimony. The author does know with certainty that Molina had direct charge of the areas where violations could have occurred and that Molina had at various times cautioned the author pertaining to proper precautions.

Ray Molina's son was a foreman under Ray. Mr.Greuling told the author that this young man could have testified to truths that would probably have cleared him (Greuling) of unfounded charges. This young man, according to Greuling' was sent with his family, at government expense, on an island cruise for a three week period during the Greuling trial.

This story is probably a thousand times more horrible than can be told by the author with the limited material available to him. Hopefully, the time will come that all the facts can be made public through the "horse's mouth". Meantime, the author can only testify that he has known these people for years and believes them to be decent, hardworking, honorable citizens who provided employment to support many families for close to forty years in their community before their government raped and destroyed them.

Along with prison, the family lost about a half million dollars of their own money and close to the same amount of investor's money. They were getting ready to open a brand new modern shop wherein new EPA regulations would be easier to comply with. All this was, of course, lost through legal costs and fines.

The author is aware that the majority of his compatriots cannot bring themselves to believe that their beloved government can be evil. They do not want to believe such things. Oh how those of us who have tasted of the persecution would like to be able to feel that way too. Truth is truth, though, and we cannot change what is. The injustices are not diminishing; they are growing by leaps and bounds. It will not be many years before all will have tasted or at least been close enough to see and smell the danger to all who have anything of value to be stolen by our government.

The author grieves for the Greulings. They did him wonderful and unselfish service for which he is deeply grateful. He can only hope they have the fortitude to come through their hardships still demonstrating the courage and honesty they used to demonstrate. The author believes that a just God will someday judge and severely punish all those who participate in such unjust persecution of lovely and innocent people.

CHAPTER 6

This narrative would be noticeably incomplete without some discussion about our *beloved* **Gestapo,** the IRS. Every man and woman in this country's work force has felt the pressures exerted by this **un-constitutional** agency. You won't be subjected here to a lengthy, yet inadequate synopsis. A brief outline with two short stories will suffice. Each and every one of you, if aware of your surroundings, know that you have brushed with similar cases. You've either had, or know someone who has had experiences similar to those described here. Dear reader, it is hoped that you don't shrug and say they probably had it coming. No citizen of any state in our Union deserves the kind of treatment dished out by this illegal **Gestapo.**

You are urged to send for the book titled, "Detaxing America" by Edmund Fitzsimmons. Contact Truth in taxation at 11022 Ventura Blvd. Suite 239, Studio City, California. Mr. Fitzsimmons did a wonderful job of describing the IRS in its position of illegally usurped power over us, the people. He insinuates that though they probably are not even a government agency, they are aided and abetted by **our** government in their illegal machinations against us. "Detaxing America" is probably the most complete, condensed accumulation of truth that you can acquire pertaining to the horrible and illegal taxation we are subjected to.

The author can only suggest that this **Gestapo** fits perfectly into the classification of un-constitutional, because it is in opposition to the rights over which our founders declared our independence. It directly controverts the spirit of, or the reasons for being, of **our** Constitution. As is so often reiterated herein, stupid, evil decisions by godless justices, do not create true constitutionality.

Reiterating once more; **any <u>law</u> or <u>decision</u> which negates or ignores the <u>spirit</u> of our Constitution, tearing down our freedoms, which were paid for in blood, are patently illegal and un-constitutional.** In plain language, no Supreme Court Justice, was ever so great and wonderful a personage as to have a right to rape and tear down our Constitution. Who do they think they are? The author is not cussing, but is rather making a personal request in vehemently exclaiming; **<u>"God, damn them."</u>**

As is put forth in "Detaxing America", the ownership of the IRS is in question. If it is (heaven forbid) owned by the US Government, someone in authority ought to show this fact to us. It has not thus far been given to us to know with certainty. We have a right to opine, in view of the absence of evidence to the contrary, that they are in fact as seems apparent, simply an appendage to the illegally operating, privately owned, Federal Reserve Bank. It is this diabolical bank that receives the blood money, collected by the IRS **Gestapo**.

The illegal **Gestapo**, called the IRS, is to the body of the people of this nation, like diabetes is to the individual. It is insidious, slowly but surely destroying the organs necessary to life. While they are enforcing only a small portion of the rape of our people, it is by itself, so large as to be a death threatening portion. They crush individuals and businesses alike to feed their ever increasing, gluttonous appetite. They hunger for your hard earned possessions and the agents tend to glory in their power over you.

Inserted here, is an observation which may help you, dear reader, to properly understand the kind of people who work for the IRS, to help with the rape of our nation.

For all of our lives we have been subjected to the wonderful world of entertainment. The movies we watch, though fictional, do to a large degree, depict the way we are, or the way we were. The author has always wondered about a phenomenon often depicted in the "Cowboys and Indians" movies. The army, usually depicted as "the good guys", invariably employed Indian scouts. These movies are seldom true accounts, but, yes, they are **based** on the way it was.

History bears out the existence of many Indians who were willing to help the US Army against their own people. **How could they** have **helped** the **enemy** to **destroy** their **own**? Hard to believe, isn't it? In truth, they were not unlike the vast number of our countrymen who have joined with the enemy in destroying the productive element of our society today. It is because of people of this ilk that the **Gestapos** can exist. The IRS couldn't be raping us as they do without these traitors that make up this diabolical agency.

If you are an observing person, you often see men justify actions harmful to others, because "it is the law." At those times, please consider the fact that many of our laws are illegal. Please remember that no law that tears down our **God-given freedom** is legal. To hell with those kind of laws and the traitors who enforce them. The IRS is an illegal entity. Those who work for this rapist are ideologically descended from the Indian scouts who helped to destroy their own people. Remember this, when you're forced to deal with them. Remember also, to whom they've sold their souls, for money.

Ervin Stene is **supposedly**, a free born citizen of the sovereign state of South Dakota. He was born in Sioux Falls, on March 1, 1946. Erve was raised on a farm, where he had the wonderful advantage denied to most of our youths today. He was raised to understand that work is a necessary and wonderful part of life. In those days gone by, our government had not yet grown so massive. Men in those days still had some sense of working for the good of their own families. Our socialistic system was in those times still in its infancy. Oppression of the producers was not nearly so prominent as it is today.

Erve grew up as did most of us, with love for, and proud of his country. He believed the teachers of his youth, who taught him that ours was a system of **free enterprise.** Like most of us, he gloried in that concept. Little did he dream that he would wear out his life with working, to end up with only a small fraction of a percent for himself and his family, of all he's produced. Little did he dream that he'd one day come on hard times and need a little time to raise money for the revenue collectors of the Federal Reserve Bank.

In youth, Erve worked hard, played hard and completed his education. He graduated from Dakota State University with a bachelor's degree. He was bitten by wanderlust, which took him to Denver, Colorado, where he became a carpenter. His next move was to Old Mexico, where he wasted some of his youth in mining ventures that didn't pay off.

Erve took a wife. Having a family to support had the natural effect on him. The responsibility of a family separates the men from the boys. Stene became a man, beginning to direct his efforts towards raising and supporting his family. Time flew as time does. Erve ended up in El Paso, Texas. By 1978, he was supporting five people. In some ways Erve is exceptional, or similar to a **minority**, among his peers. He is fiercely independent. He is the perfect example of the entrepreneur who cannot be otherwise.

Erve goes to bed scheming and theming, as entrepreneurs do and rises the same way, sorting out and organizing his tasks for the day. Most employees have the luxury of being directed. People like Erve have to do the directing.

To make a long story short, Erve is the typical hardworking, small, American business man who earns his way with his sweat. Of course, among his *chief desires is to be hounded and harassed* by **Gestapo** agents, who have no idea what real work is. One would expect him to have strong feelings of *endearment* towards men who earn more than he does by controlling and manipulating his life and efforts.

The IRS agent that took Erves case was named Hunter. He was a man as would make **Gestapo** heads proud. He had the ability to smoothly sweet talk his victims while extracting all useful information needed for their harassment. After acquisition of all useful information, Hunter could then be hatefully vicious, harassing with veiled threats of the terrible things he could impose on *fools* in debt to the IRS.

Erve Stene didn't try to cheat them. Because he is intelligent, he knows instinctively that they have no moral right to his earnings. Also, because he is intelligent, he understands the futility of trying to keep his earnings for his family. He knows the IRS has the mighty un-constitutional government behind them to crush him if he fails to do homage.

As always, Erve filed his IRS tax return for the year of 1984. It had been a tough year. Although on paper he showed a small profit, he had no money. Knowing better than to try cheating, he filed, showing a tax liability. He then made arrangements to pay the debt with interest, of course. Erve had receivables at that time that would cover the taxes when these receivables were realized. He showed Hunter, evidence of his ability to pay, upon receipt of these funds. Hunter agreed to wait the **three weeks** for Erve to pay.

Of course, one would *expect* an IRS agent to *keep his word*, right? Don't be foolish. The kind of people who will work for oppressive agencies have no integrity. Men and women, willing to oppress their fellow men, are immoral. The truth is not in them. Don't trust them. They are bad people, lacking in human kindness and unable to correctly judge between right and wrong. These IRS agents try to shame us, the producers, while they themselves are truly the dregs of society. They are leeches, living off the sweat of the honest producers of the wealth of our nation.

Who can say what makes this kind of man tick? Why would he agree to wait the short time, then change his mind and break his word? There seems to be no rhyme nor reason for the actions of our Godless overseers. Ideological, Indian scout descendant, Hunter, sweetly agreed to wait for Erve to collect money with which to pay his tax debt (about 1400.00). A few days later, Hunter and his cohorts, swooped in to show their power.

Rosie pulled up to drop one of the children at school. With her were Carlos, 16, Amy, 10, Elmer, 7, and Erve's 77 year old mother. Who knows what possessed **Gestapo** agents to track down the wife, mother and children, so to speak, in a public place. Why not simply go to their home to rip away their property?

117

Two cars pinned her into the parking space in front of the school. Out piled **Gestapo** agents, flashing badges and assuring Rosie that they were all powerful. They took her car. They were *kind*, though, or *magnanimous*. They gave the frightened and humiliated family a ride home.

You cannot feel the intensity of his family's horror, unless you are able to visualize yourself in their shoes. This was Erve's family that he loved, being frightened and mistreated in public, by what he thought were **his** government's representatives. Who knows what he'd have done had he been there. A good many men, had it been their family, and had they been there and armed, might have taken some lives. Had Erve done this, he'd have been touted as a foul murderer.

Fortunately for Erve and his family, their mistreatment didn't bring about violence, nor was it contemplated. One can begin to understand though, how many of our countrymen are being driven beyond their breaking point. Being abused without good cause and being helpless to react is terribly frustrating. It is easy to see why men crack under the strain and why some go berserk, losing control of themselves and committing unspeakable crimes.

The author is opposed to violence. He would not go so far though, as to suggest cowardly aquiecence to attack on one's person or property. Self defense is a **God given** right. It is a lack of willingness to defend ourselves that gives the criminals the courage to destroy us or that which we've worked for. Having a **Gestapo** badge does not make the bearer any less criminal when he damages one without **just** cause. Hiding behind corrupt laws or agencies does not make one or one's actions any less criminal.

Lets move on to the trials suffered by Murray Voight, at the hands of the IRS **Gestapo**. Murray is a citizen of Texas and is a productive, hard working member of that state's mainstay supporters. He is part of the less than half of our work force that produces the goods and services necessary to support the majority who work for our great oppressive government.

Murray, an entrepreneur, does computer programming, consulting and general service work. Without him and others like him, America's offices would squeak to a halt. We are a computerized nation. Without people like Murray, we'd have to go back to calculators and typewriters.

One would think that a brilliant programmer would use a good accounting program and would keep perfect books. From such books, his income tax filing could be prepared easily and accurately. The problem with Murray is that he's like most of us. He puts his energies into his area of expertise. He leaves to accountants, the distasteful job of analyzing his business and filing his returns with the illegal and cruel IRS **Gestapo**.

No accountant can understand the details of your business like you can; neither are any of them perfectly faultless. Accountants make mistakes too. Some are better than others. The luck of the draw went against Murray Voight in selecting an accountant to prepare his tax returns for 1987, 1988 and 1989.

When the hated IRS audited, they disallowed some of his deductions. They decided that he should have paid more taxes than his accountant had determined. You must remember that accountants require that you absolve them from responsibility for errors. If **they** slip up, **you** pay the price. Like doctors and lawyers, they charge exorbitantly and guarantee nothing.

Of course, you would *expect* the IRS to *recognize* simple error and to collect the blood money *gently*. You might expect this if you and yours never dealt with them. Murray Voight will never again expect from them, fair or sympathetic treatment.

Constitutional Law requires that direct taxes such as income tax be voluntary. We are no longer governed by Constitutional Law. The blood suckers were true to form with the Voights. They decided that he owed 21,000.00. This was determined to be owed by him for a three year period. They naturally included penalties and then charged interest (usury) on top of it all. Murray must have been *overjoyed* at the demands of those that he had thought to be *public servants.*

The Voights didn't have that kind of money on hand. They arranged to make monthly payments to the *beloved* rapists of American Society. The payment schedule was agreed to. One would expect this to be the end of persecution, if Murray made the payments on time. It does not work that way. When you deal with people who are willing to turn on and harass their own, you must expect constant, repetitive agitation.

A business, small, or large, has operational expenses. One cannot remain in business if one cannot pay the bills. As pointed out, arrangements were made for payments. The IRS then swooped in to confiscate his bank account. Pretty nice, eh! You must pay us while we make it next to impossible for you to operate. Twice, during the course of six months, The **Gestapo** emptied his bank account, while he made all payments on time.

The **Gestapo** also liened his home and even started possession proceedings. In Texas this is illegal. Even the feared IRS **Gestapo** is not supposed to be able to **legally** take a Texas Homestead. The IRS cares nothing about legality. They did start the action. In an appeal hearing he proved that his payments had all been made on time. The action to take his home was forestalled, but the lien is still in place. Once again, this is not legal in Texas.

Unless one has seen the IRS **Gestapo** in action, first hand, one will have difficulty in believing that things like this can take place. Look around you. Talk to your friends and neighbors. You'll find it to be much more prevalent than you might have thought possible.

Murray's ordeal is not over. He has to make payments until January of the year 2001. Would that it were as simple as in the days of Robin Hood. It is not though, and we, the people, face much more suffering before this, *our* government and the many **Gestapos** it sponsors are set straight.

CHAPTER 7

You have been subjected to a good deal of negativity thus far in these musings. Negativity is not the intent, but truth is. If you can see the truth, you can, if you will, be a part of correcting the problems. They can be corrected. They will be rectified. The injustices described here are not even a drop in the bucket. They are but a drop in the ocean. On every hand, man's injustice to man is evident. A society will eventually emerge, however, wherein glorious freedom will exist. The beauty of peace and joy will replace the pain and sorrow. Equity will be won for all. There will be a cleanup. Those who are left will inherit a different world.

When God destroyed Sodom and Gamorrah, he did so based on his guarantee to mankind of a **"right" to life, liberty and the pursuit of happiness.** The fact is that if a society is completely evil and vile, no good and healthy thing can, from thence, sally forth.

The scriptures tell us that all things were created first in the spirit before the world was. Scriptures in which most of us claim belief tell us that our physical state is but a step in an eternal journey. The Israelitish beliefs of old were to the effect that there will indeed be life after death. The belief was that the spirit separation from the soul which comes at death is temporary (spirit being plus the physical body equals a soul). A resurrection or a reuniting of spirit with physical bodies was predicted.[18]

By the time that Jesus the Christ came on the scene, many of the Israelites had become much like ourselves. Many had begun to doubt the old teachings. Most of the Israelitish nation had, of course, long since dispersed. Much of the tribe of Benjamin and many of the Levites remained with Judah in the promised land, which we know as Israel. These two and a half tribes are numbered together and are hated, loved, tolerated or admired by us all as Jews. They are Caucasians and cousins to all Caucasians on this planet. The dispersed tribes, ten in number, lost their identity by scattering or being scattered, far and wide. They've co-mingled with the rest of the world.

All the tribes of Israel were together as God led them out of the land of Egypt where they had been enslaved. God had made promises to their fathers, to Abraham, Isaac and Jacob. He'd promised that their seed would be blessed and that He would be their God and protect them. Don't become upset and jealous of

---

[18] Romans 8:11

the special place of Israel with God. Remember that all the righteous become Israelites by adoption. This is to the author, the greatest part of the promise to Abraham, that he will be known as the father to all the righteous. Remember also, that promises of blessings from God are always contingent upon some reciprocating action on our part.

In 1250, BC, with **God's** help, Moses led the children of Israel out of Egypt. While they were still in the wilderness, **God** spoke to all Israel from a cloud covering. All Israel did hear and fear and did make covenant with **God**. The agreement was that they would keep His **law of liberty**, thereby guaranteeing freedom to themselves and their posterity. **God** promised that if they would do so, He would protect and nurture Israel. He also told them though, that if they trampled His law under-foot, refusing to honor it and respect their neighbors rights, that He, **God,** would turn his face against them. He said in this case that He would allow their enemies to conquer and abuse them. This happened to ten of the tribes in 722, BC. They were conquered and dispersed, soon losing their identity, mingling with Shem's other decendents and those of Japeth and Ham. Japeth is father to the Asiatics and Ham became father to the descendants of Cain, or the Canaanites. Shem's children are the Caucasian races.

Because they had for their civil law, their constitution, the **Law of God,** the ***Perfect Law of Liberty,*** Judah became the greatest power on earth, for a time. Judah (Jews, Levites and Benjaminites) remained the envy, the strongest and wealthiest nation on earth until about 600 BC, when **God** kept his promise to turn away from them. When they abandoned Him and his **Laws**, He turned aside, allowing their enemies to overcome them temporarily. He had mercy though, and did not entirely forsake Israel. He did, from time to time, restore at least, some of their greatness. He has promised to do this again in these last days.

Perhaps the greatest punishment to Israel for their stiff necked, hard hearted, abandonment of the **Law of Liberty**, was the withdrawing by **God** of His Spirit. Please read the scripture[19] *Blindness in part hath happened to Israel until the fullness of the Gentiles shall be brought in. I, the Lord God will bring strong delusion. I will not always strive with man.*[20] These punishments are of course, self inflicted. The **Lord God**, being the author of truth, must keep His word to leave us to our own devices when we abandon Him and His **law**. It is certainly a form of punishment, but at the same time, our "Father, **God**," in his mercy, is to a

---

[19] Romans 11:25
[20] Genesis 6:3

degree, blessing us by giving us smaller, or weaker emanations of His Spirit. Because He is just, He cannot punish us for ignorance.

Where there is no law, there is no condemnation. We, of course, harm ourselves, but **God** is not duty bound to punish us as harshly while His Spirit is withdrawn. Don't you believe that the withdrawing of the Spirit has ever been complete. Every man and woman has the ability to pick up the emanations, through exercise of the principles which activate the receiver. Use the key. Seek and ye shall find. The withdrawing of **God's** Spirit is never absolute. It is simply less intense so that only those who want and seek it, will, by it be blessed.

The author believes that now, in the last days, **God** will extend the greatest dispensation of mercy the world has ever known. Because He partially withdrew His spirit and because He is just, He will, accordingly, extend great mercy.

For the most part, **God** has left man to his own devices. This is what we mostly want. We want the free agency to pick and choose for ourselves, the type of beings we will be. Our free agency was agreed to in the heavens before our earthly habitat was prepared. **God** agreed to extend free agency to us. By His own law, He cannot interfere until we become so awful that children cannot grow up among us with freedom to choose other than evil.

Children cannot choose righteousness if they're never exposed to it. When societies are ripened in iniquity, when nations become completely corrupted, then in justice, they must be destroyed. In this way, previously created spirits can come to earth with some chance for freedom. **God** guarantees freedom; we fight against him, usurping illegal control over one another. This is dangerously idiotic, because, He agreed to take a hand. It is the height of arrogance to believe that we can indefinitely expropriate our fellow man's rights. **God** must eventually halt such proceedings.

By the time Christ appeared, the Jewish nation was again bickering and contending over its old teachings. The Pharisees believed in the old teachings about pre-existence. They believed in the concept of the spirit uniting with the physical body to form a soul. The Pharisees believed in the ultimate resurrection, or re-unification in the future of spirit bodies with physical, of all who had lived and died. This was not a new idea with Christ. It had been taught from the foundation of the world forward.

At that time, the Jewish nation had in some ways become similar to ourselves, at this time. There was a great diversity of beliefs. The Sadducees believed the resurrection teachings to be a bunch of hooey. Spirituality was at a low ebb. The Jews in great numbers were becoming unwilling to accept teachings on faith. Faith is belief in things evidenced, but not seen. Contentions over belief in the resurrection were a long way from being the only differences among that people. Historians depict them as being an argumentative populous that squabbled and harangued constantly.

The "old ways", the "old beliefs", were laughed at by many of the youth. In large numbers they accepted *Gods* other than their own. **Filthy Lucre** (money) became very important to that people. In their arrogance, they began to scrutinize the size of families raised by their fellows. They began to scorn men who took multiple wives and raised "too many" children. Celcis, an accredited historian of that day, said that the young Rabbi, Jesus, was despised because of the number of his wives and children. Rabbis, of course, had to be married, nor could a man by law, handle another's children if he had none of his own. *Shouldn't* a man though, limit the size of his family to comply with the desires of his fellows?

Greed at that day was prevalent, as was arrogance, pride, power mongery and sexual immorality. Of course, these criminal tendencies developed over time. It took till about 90 AD before **God** had, according to His covenant, finally abandoned these last identifiable Israelites to their own devices. Rome finally drove the Jews from their homeland. They scattered throughout the world.

The Jews have retained a little of their old spirituality. One of the more important of their laws, they've kept pretty religiously. The **Lord God** commanded the children of Israel, not to mix their seed with others than their own family. Intermarriage with outsiders was strictly forbidden. They've been harshly criticized for this regulation. Anyone critical of the Jews for their refusal to intermarry with outsiders, should be ashamed. The Jews, in this, are only obeying **God's** law.

Well, onto that scene of contentious bickering and disagreement, came Jesus. He made some claims which seemed outrageous to most Jews. Remember please, that he found great acceptance to a point. The books of Mathew and Mark say that all Jerusalem went out unto John's baptism.[21] John baptized in the name of Jesus Christ.

A great deal had been predicted about a great prophet, a son of **God**, that would come unto Israel. Many attributes and actions were imputed unto him by the prophets with clarity. This Jesus Christ seemed in many ways to fulfill the

---

[21] Matthew 3:5-6, Mark 1:5

predictions. He did not, though, by a long shot, fill all the expectations as set forth by Israelitish scripture. Even most Christians agree that he did not come in the capacity of the Messiah.

According to prophecy, the Messiah will come in a cloud of glory and will go before Israel with the armies of heaven. He will, per scriptures, free Israel from bondage. The Messiah will take the reins of political power and will reign as King over the whole earth.

We, citizens of the USA and of earth, have for a time, seen efforts of proponents of **one-world** government. This does not refer to **God's** effort to establish His Kingdom with the Messiah at the helm. The present organization of **one-worlders** look primarily for absolute, economic control. Of course, to maintain their aims, they will need military might, or police power. A **one-world** government is not such a bad idea. If the head of government and the officials were guided by the spirit of **God**, it would be a much less complicated and a better world to live in. These money powers, however, who are trying to control the world are servants, not of **God**, but of Lucifer, the Old Devil, the Son of the Morning.

Scripture tells us that Lucifer, with one-third of the hosts of heaven, made war on **God** and the rest of us. He lost the war and was cast to earth to roam in his spirit form, never to receive a physical body like you and yours have. Just as **God** sends prophets to help those of us who will receive them, the arch enemy, Lucifer, has his high priests. The great high priest for Satan, he who stands in the office like that held for **God** by Moses, Christ and others, is Master Mahan.

God called men like Noah, Abraham, Moses, Christ and a few others through whom to dispense His blessings to the human family. Lucifer has also, through the ages, sent his prophets. Satan and his disciples seem to be winning the battle for converts. The Devil's prime motivator is the subjugation of man to his power. Absolute control of man through force is his aim.

Maybe it is necessary for us to see the mess made by men led by Lucifer, so that we can intelligently make our choice. The world is a mess. The United States of America is the leader of the world. We are the only entity at this time which fills the description to a **T**, of the great **Babylon**, described in the book of Revelations.[22] We are described there as the whore of all the earth, who has fornicated with the kings of the earth and have purchased the wares of all nations.

---

[22] Revelations chapter 18

This book says that ships at sea will stay afar off for fear of the smoke of our burning.

Among you, sectarians, exist a variety of ideas about who this **Babylon** might be. Howl you sectarians, weep and wail and rend your cloths. Lucifer has you under his thumb. The USA fits perfectly the description of the latter day **Babylon,** and is in fact, that exceedingly wicked nation. Read the chapter for yourself. Read it prayerfully, exercising the key for discernment of truth. You will learn the truth thereby.

Pay close attention to the scripture; verse 4 of the 18th chapter of Revelations. It says; *Come out of her my people, that you be not partakers of her plagues.* If you choose to mystify the scriptures, it is your choice. Most of them are more correctly interpreted literally. They say what they mean and mean what they say. Give yourself over to soothsayers, false priests or psychics. Let them lead you. Let them mystify the **Word of God** for you and enroll or keep you in Lucifer's army. The alternative is for you to pray for yourself, decide for yourself, act for yourself, be your own person. Study and pray seeking the Spirit that permeates the whole universe. Choose to honor the glorious position that is yours for the taking. Be a deserving and willing Child of **God**.

Come, let us reason together. Would a loving father, a **God**, create children in His Own Image, then relax contentedly while they fight, bicker and usurp power over one another? Would such a **One** do nothing to help His children to grow into capable, strong individuals who would love and help one another? Could such a Being create a world for his children and offer it only to a few of them, granting power to that few to use all others for their own gratification and aggrandizement? No! These things do not come from **God**. This world, in its present state, is following our **God's** arch enemy. We are following and assisting him who is warring against our **God**. Shame on us all. We refuse to do homage to Him who gave us life and we follow instead, His enemy, who cares nothing for us. As children of a **Living God**, created in His image, we fall far short of our potential. It does not appear that we are deserving of much help from our **Father**.

Coming back to these men, Christ and the Messiah, certain scriptures will be listed, which describe them both. These are predictions of the prophets who spoke of the coming of them both in terms that can be confusing, but understandable, if you will obtain the still small voice that whispereth understanding.

Isaiah 7: 14 says: *Therefore the Lord himself shall give you a sign; Behold a virgin shall conceive, and bear a son, and shall call his name Immanuel.*

The book of Deuteronomy, chapter 18, verse 15 says: *The Lord thy **God** will raise up unto thee a Prophet from the midst of thee, of thy bretheren like unto me: unto him ye shall hearken.* A prophet like unto Moses would be great indeed. We see in Deuteronomy 34:10 that: *And there arose not a prophet since in Israel like Moses, whom the Lord knew face to face.*

Daniel 9:25-27 says: *25 Know therefore and understand that from the going forth of the commandment to restore and to build Jerusalem unto the Messiah the Prince shall be seven weeks and threescore and two weeks: the street shall be built again, and the wall, even in troublous times. 26 And after threescore and two weeks shall Messiah be cut off, but not for himself: and the people of the prince that shall come shall destroy the city and the sanctuary; and the end thereof shall be with a flood, and unto the end of the war desolations are determined. 27 And he shall confirm the covenant with many for one week: and in the midst of the week he shall cause the sacrifice and oblation to cease, and for the overspreading of abominations he shall make it desolate, even until the consummation, and that determined shall be poured upon the desolate.*

Acts 3:20-23 *20 And he shall send Jesus Christ, which before was preached unto you: 21 Whom the heaven must receive until the times of restitution of all things, which **God** hath spoken by the mouth of all his holy prophets since the world began. 22 For Moses truly said unto the fathers; A prophet shall ye hear in all things whatsoever he shall say unto you.*

John 1:41 says: *He first findeth his own brother Simon, and saith unto him, We have found the "Messias, which is being interpreted, the Christ."*

John 4:25-26 *25 The woman saith unto him, I know that "Messias cometh, which is called Christ: when he is come, he will tell us all things. 26 Jesus saith unto her, "I that speak unto thee am he."*

Romans 11: 26 *And so all Israel shall be saved: as it is written, There shall come out of Sion the Deliverer, and shall turn away ungodliness from Jacob.*

Isaiah 59:20 *And the redeemer shall come to Zion, and unto them that turn from transgression in Jacob, saith the Lord.*

The 53rd chapter of Isaiah is presented for the reader's discernment as to whom this chapter refers: *Who hath believed our report? And to whom is the arm of the Lord revealed? 2 For he shall grow up before him as a tender plant, and as a root out of a dry ground: he hath no form nor comeliness; and when we shall see him, there is no beauty that we should desire him. 3 He is despised and rejected of men; a man of sorrows, and acquainted with grief: and we hid as it were our faces from him; he was despised, and we esteemed him not. 4 Shurely he hath borne our griefs, and carried our sorrows: yet we did esteem him stricken, smitten of God, and afflicted. 5 But he was wounded for our transgressions, he was bruised for our iniquities: the chastisement of our peace was upon him: and with his stripes we are healed. 6 All we like sheep have gone astray; we have turned every one to his own way; and the Lord hath laid on him the iniquity of us all. 7 He was oppressed and he was afflicted, yet he opened not his mouth: he is brought as a lamb to the slaughter, and as a sheep before her shearers is dumb, so he openeth not his mouth. 8 He was taken from prison and from judgment: and who shall declare his generation? For he was cut off out of the land of the living: for the transgression of my people was he stricken. 9 And he made his grave with the wicked, and with the rich in his death; because he had done no violence, neither was any deceit in his mouth, 10 Yet it pleased the Lord to bruise him; he hath put him to grief: when thou shalt make his soul an offering for sin, he shall see his seed, he shall prolong his days, and the pleasure of the Lord shall prosper in his hand. 11 He shall see the travail of his soul, and shall be satisfied: by his knowledge shall my righteous servant justify many; for he shall bear their iniquities. 12 Therefore will I divide him a portion with the great, and he shall divide the spoil with the strong; because he hath poured out his soul unto death: and he was numbered with the transgressors; and he bare the sin of many, and made intercession for the transgressors.*

You may also, dear reader, decide who is referred to in Micah 5: 1-2 *Now gather thyself in troops, O daughter of troops: he hath laid siege against us: they shall smite the judge of Israel with a rod upon the cheek. 2 But thou, Bethlehem Ephrata, though thou be little among the thousands of Judah, yet out of thee shall he come forth unto me that is to be ruler in Israel; whose goings forth have been from of old, from everlasting.*

Last, but not least, you are asked to read the 14th chapter of Zachariah, comparing this prophecy to the foregoing: *BEHOLD, the day of the Lord cometh, and thy spoil shall be divided in the midst of thee. 2 For I will gather all nations against Jerusalem to battle; and the city shall be taken, and the houses rifled, and the women ravished; and half of the city shall go forth into captivity, and the residue of the people shall not be cut off from the city. 3 Then shall the Lord go forth, and fight against those nations, as when he fought in the day of the battle. 4 And his feet shall stand in that day upon the mount of Olives, which is before Jerusalem on the east and the mount of Olives shall cleave in the midst thereof toward the east and toward the west, and there shall be a very great valley; and half of the mountain shall remove toward the north, and half of it toward the south. 5 And ye shall flee to the valley of the mountains; for the valley of the mountains shall reach unto A'zal: Yea, ye shall flee, like as ye fled from before the earthquake in the days of Uzzi'ah king of Judah: and the Lord my God shall come, and all the saints with thee. 6 And it shall come to pass in that day, that the light shall not be clear, nor dark: 7 But it shall be one day which shall be known to the Lord, not day, nor night: but it shall come to pass, that at evening time it shall be light. 8 And it shall be in that day, that living waters shall go out from Jerusalem; half of them toward the former sea, and half of them toward the hinder sea in summer and in winter shall it be. 9 And the Lord shall be king over all the earth: in that day shall there be one Lord, and his name one. 10 All the land shall be turned as a plain from Ge'ba to Remmon south of Jerusalem: and it shall be lifted up and inhabited in her place, from Benjamin's gate into the place of the first gate, unto the corner gate, and from the tower of Hanan'eel unto the king's winepresses. 11 And men shall dwell in it, and there shall be no more utter destruction; but Jerusalem shall be safely inhabited. 12 And this shall be the plague wherewith the Lord will smite all the people that have fought against Jerusalem; Their flesh shall consume away while they stand upon their feet, and their eyes shall consume away in their holes, and their tongue shall consume away in their mouth. 13 And it shall come to pass in that day that a great tumult from the Lord shall be among them; and they shall lay hold every one on the hand of his neighbour, and his hand shall rise up against the hand of his neighbour. 14 And Judah also shall fight at Jerusalem; and the wealth of all the heathen round about shall be gathered together, gold and silver, and apparel, in great abundance. 15 And so shall be the plague of the horse, of the mule, of the camel, and of the ass, and of all the beasts that shall be in these tents, as this plague. And it shall come to pass, that every one that is left of all the nations which came against Jerusalem shall even go up from year to year to worship the King, the Lord of hosts, and to keep the feast of tabernacles. 17*

And it shall be, that whoso will not come up of all the families of the earth unto Jerusalem to worship the King, the Lord of hosts, even upon them shall be no rain. 18 And if the family of Egypt go not up, and come not, that have no rain; there shall be the plague, wherewith the Lord will smite the heathen that come not up to keep the feast of tabernacles. 19 This shall be the punishment of Egypt, and the punishment of all nations that come not up to keep the feast of tabernacles. 20 In that day shall there be upon the bells of the horses HOLINESS UNTO THE LORD; and the pots in the Lord's house shall be like the bowls before the altar. 21 Yea, every pot in Jerusalem and in Judah shall be holiness unto the Lord of hosts: and all they that sacrifice shall come and take of them, and seethe therein: and in that day there shall be no more the canaanite in the house of the Lord of hosts.

Will you contend that Christ filled all the requirements, as predicted.? You won't if you are willing to accept the scriptures for what they say. Neither can you argue though, that he didn't fulfill a great portion of the prophecies. Is it just possible that he may have told the truth about himself? He maintained that before He could rise above all things, He was required first to descend below all things. Before He could be a leader of men in a complete sense, He had first to serve them. If you prayerfully read the scriptures which predict the coming of Christ and then study His life, you will agree that the office or position of a Christ, was fulfilled by Jesus.

Reading the scriptures pertaining to the things to be done by Messiah, will convince any halfwit, that the Messianic Office or work, has not been accomplished. Jesus Christ did not take the reins of political power, as is prophesied that the Messiah will do. He did not go ahead of Israel with the hosts of the armies of heaven. He did not appear in a cloud of glory, to fight the battles of his people and to establish, once and for all, **liberty** for man.

Those of you, Christians and Jews, who continue to worry and contend over the positions of Christ and the Messiah are wasting your efforts. You are beating your brains out for nothing. The Messiah will come; make no mistake about that. Who do you think he will accept as his people? Maybe the Christians who have hated and even killed Jews in the name of Christ? The fact that Christ was a Jew causes one to think that he may take a dim view of Jew haters.

Our belief as to whether Jesus filled the office of Christ and that the Messiah will be another personage, or whether both positions were to be fulfilled by the same Son of **God**, is for each of us to determine for ourselves. If the Old Testament Scriptures that predict his or their coming are false, then it's all hooey anyway. If on the other hand, these scriptures are true, then any and all, who discriminate in the name of Christ or the Messiah are hypocrites and liars. They are neither Christian nor Jew, but are disciples of Satan, charter members of his minions.

The author has his own private beliefs. He couldn't care less though, if you accept that the Messiah came as Christ and will return as the Messiah. He couldn't care less if you believe that Christ was a good man, maybe a prophet, but that the Messiah will be a different man. This much is for sure, if you are not tolerant of other's beliefs and willing to respect other's views and rights, neither Christ, nor the Messiah, nor Christ Messiah, will accept you in his or their camp.

When the Messiah comes, he will show us scars from wounds in his hands, or he won't. Whether he does or does not, those of us who are worthy to be called his friends, will be accepted as such by him. This worthiness will depend on one thing only, how have we treated our fellow man. If you think for one minute, that you can cheat your neighbor, steal from him, usurp unjust power over him and still be counted as a friend of **God**, Christ, Messiah, or Christ Messiah, guess again. You will not be recognized as friend to any of them unless you have kept the **Law**.

Come, let us reason together. You are strong, or you are weak. You are good, or you are bad. You Love **Liberty** and are willing to fight for it, for yourself and your fellows, or you do not care. If you'd rather rule over others, take from them the fruits of their labor, you have been well described earlier in these writings. In this case, you have chosen your side in the coming crisis, the impending battle. If you've chosen Lucifer and his ways, you have a great deal of company. You are in the majority. You will not win though, in the long run. You will weep and wail.

During the great and terrible destructions that we are bringing down upon our own heads, one thing only will separate and save those few who will be saved. Willingness to accept the ***Perfect Law of Liberty*** is the requirement. This **Law**, as summed up in the **Ten Commandments**, basically requires respect for your neighbor's **God**-given rights. If this respect, this love of **God's Law**, is truly in your heart, you will be accepted into the coming "Free Society."

In Holy Writ are found various terms for the phenomenon that is to take place. The separation of the sheep from the goats, the separation of the wheat from the tares, the gathering of Israel, are a few colloquialisms. *Come out of her my people*, is the cry. Would **God** send this message, yet fail to prepare a gathering place for His people? Not likely! He will prepare a Zion. He will establish a place of refuge where the honest in heart can live in peace and tranquility. This has been promised. God does not lie.[23]

The following song expresses perfectly and beautifully, today's most appropriate message to Israel.

---

[23] Numbers 23:19, Deuteronomy 32: 4, Hebrews 6:18, Titus 1:2

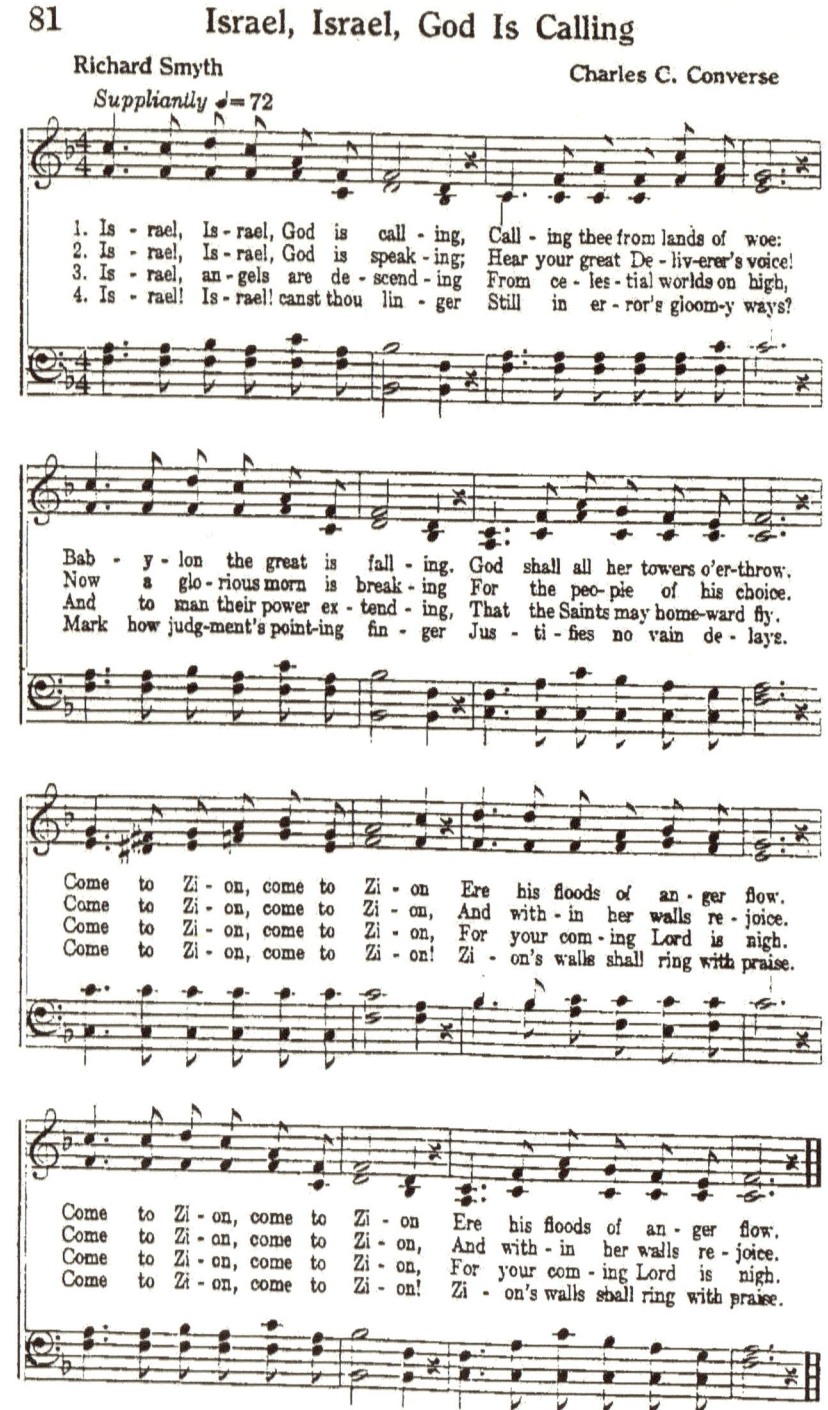

81 Israel, Israel, God Is Calling

We live in terrible times, yet for those who make the right choice, the great adventure is just ahead. Some of us can have the opportunity to help re-establish **freedom**, to build Utopia. Didn't you ever in youth, dream of adventurous times? Didn't you kind of wish you'd been born when great events were taking place? Yes, we are coming to the end times, as prophesied from the beginning of our race (Adam's family) upon this Earth. These will truly be the "times to try men's souls." For those who make the right choice though, it will be high adventure.

This treatise has described a very tiny portion of the evils of our government. To look at all the methods in which its members infringe upon our **liberty** would waste too much time. Those of you who can be called the honest in heart, those of you who don't have your heads buried in the sand, know these things to be true.

If you can discern truth, you know also that this corrupt government has caused the formation of a great variety of opposition. The human being is a reactive animal. We know instinctively that we have a right to freedom, and the stronger souls will always fight for it. Groups have been forming all over this land, Patriots, Skin Heads, Neo-Nazis, Klu-Klux-Klanners and who knows how many more. These groups have seen the injustice, the evil dispensed by our corrupted government. It would go against nature for these government opposing groups not to form. They are the natural effect of the cause. The gangs, the druggies and the entire lawless element, are the direct and natural result of our lawless government.

Knowing that the gangs, the independent criminals, the organized, lawless groups are a natural result, a created reality, does not diminish in the least, the suffering they do and will cause. Only the "blind, following the blind," can fail to see that these groups are as criminal as is our government. Murdering the innocent, bombing trains, ripping off or stealing from armored cars, banks or stores, are not legitimate under any guise. If you can justify these actions, you may as well simplify your life and join with the so called, legitimite law enforcement groups.

Most of those who join with law enforcement, be it federal, state, county or city level groups, do so to legitimize their desire to push others around. A few may do so, simply because it seems an easy and secure position, economically. Most though, glory in positions of authority over their fellow man and this is their prime motivator. Those who become active in the outlaw groups, such as Skin Heads, Neo-Nazis, Klu-Klux-Klanners, are not much different. The main difference is that the government openly extorts resources from the producers to support its henchmen. You other outlaw groups steal from us directly or from those who've stolen from us, so that they'll have to steal more, to replace what you steal. It seems an eternal round.

Where will it end? Why, it will end in the destruction of life as we know it. The government will not back down. You opposition groups won't either. You all are evily corrupt. You all will continue to bleed the meek, the producers, till there's not enough of them to support you. Yes, they'll one day quit. More and more they (the producers) will withhold their support from you, the usurpers. Those who can't hide away their meager means will simply give up and stop producing them. It's coming soon and sooner, the end of our corrupted system.

More and more, support will be withheld. The people of this nation are sick of paying more and more, while awakening to the fact that we have no security. The people are sick of watching *our* **non**-representative government **grow and glut and grow.** We're sick of seeing our efforts squandered by those who had **nothing** to do with producing our needs. Tired to death we are, of watching lying politicians beat their chests and rail about all the wondrous things they will do for us. The people are sick of paying their all to support law enforcement agencies who mainly persecute and harass the innocent who are supporting them.

More and more the people are withdrawing their support and joining with the groups who are also evil, but are at least fighting back. These groups, mobs, these gangs of men, will increase that which has begun, a totally anarchic reign, throughout our land. Yes, you disenchanted souls have been oppressed. Yes, you are reacting to oppression. No, you are not reacting in an intelligent manner, which could correct our country's ills. Yes, you will succeed in destroying our evil government. No, you will not do any more good than has this government that you will tear down.

Ours will not be an organized revolution, with one side facing off against another. We are, in fact, already in the midst of the "helter skelter" revolt that will not be halted. Before this is over, the majority of US citizens will be dead. The murders of Randy Weaver's son and wife, the Waco and the Oklahoma City massacres were skirmishes that truly show us that the government will not back down without a fight.

Do you really think McVeigh and Nichols blew up that federal building from outside? The author does not have perfect knowledge of that incident. Most of us have only news media accounts. They, mostly of course, give us what they're given by our glorious **Gestapos**. Of course, they've made it look bad for the accused. One thing they cannot ever do is to pre-fabricate truth. "Something is rotten in Denmark."

The author does not "know all" about explosives. He did use ammonium nitrate in mining ventures long ago. Mining, excavating and road building operations all over the world use this material. It is not some deep, dark, secretive weapon known only to a few underworld blackguards. It is a high nitrogen content, chemical fertilizer, which when soaked in diesel fuel, becomes a slow burning explosive. It takes an explosive charge such as dynamite to ignite this slow burner.

A truck load of sodium nitrate placed throughout the various floors of the building might have accomplished close to the amount of damage done. Igniting it outside and several feet away from the federal building just couldn't have done extensive structural damage. Broken glass, yes. A few deaths, maybe. Concussion surely can kill. The federal building in Oklahoma City must have been blown from inside.

Of course, it is logical that the fifteen or so BATF agents housed in that building stayed away on that day. Of course, it is logical that three of them (supposedly) went in that morning, then left? It is *logical* too, that our Congress is strengthening anti-terrorist laws because of this inside job. Giving more power to the enemies of our Constitution, is of course, *more important* than the Constitution itself.

Well, of course, everyone is not fooled. More and more of our citizenry is joining the ranks of the "Helter Skelter" army of disorganized, anarchic, revolutionaries. It is logical and natural reaction for subjugated people to rebel. Unless united and guided by the **Spirit of God**, this rebellion is doomed to failure. Success will be yours to the extent that you will destroy our government, but you will also destroy yourselves in the process.

Men will travel in gangs or mobs, from town to town, raping, looting, murdering, burning, committing brigandage. Maggots will eat the flesh off of the dead bodies, too numerous to bury. Starvation will be prevalent. Cannibalism will be commonplace. Some will eat their own children before they die themselves. These things will not take place only in Washington, DC. These will be general occurrences all over this nation.

Defending ourselves is legitimate and even required by the **Law of Liberty**. Going forth in vengeance is not legitimate. In these last days, those who go forth to destroy will do so, but will also be destroyed. Thus shall the evil empire become but a memory in the minds of freemen.

All will not perish. The **Lord God** has declared that he will gather Israel and will establish a refuge, a city of peace, in these, the last days. Don't accept the word of this tiny voice. Study your scriptures. Pray to your **God**. Learn the **truth** and the **truth** will make you **free**. The **truth** will make you **free** if you take it to heart and **act** upon it.

The last days are the last of these times that Satanic powers will be allowed to exercise dominion over those who will merit **freedom** by their own resolve and actions. Those who merit **freedom** are not those who will go forth to participate in the carnage and bloodshed of their fellow citizens. No battle has ever been fought in righteousness except that it be in self defense, or if it has been commanded by **God**. If commanded by **God**, you may rest assured that He will send one or more prophets. He will also have intensified His spirit, sufficiently, that His people will recognize it and the prophets.

If you jump into the fray, participating in the carnage, you will be excluding yourself from a rightful inheritance with Israel in Zion. Yes, we must all choose for ourselves, finally. Israel will by gathered. **God** has **decreed** it.

Many hundreds of thousands of the honest in heart will gather to Zion, not because of religiosity, but for safety and because they would not take up the sword against their neighbor. They will be so numerous that there will, for a time, be danger of famine. Many will come with nothing but the clothes on their back to escape the calamities. This will be the only escape. Those who gather will try to keep Zion's **Laws**, for they will see her unity and the greatness of her organization.

This gathering out to Zion will preserve a people who will return and rebuild after the almost total destruction of our land. The entire world will, of course, be in a chaotic state. The world will have lost its market, the great and wealthy USA. The merchants of the world will lament. The banks of the world will naturally fail with our fall. The paper money system, which is controlled by the Federal Reserve Bank, will have simply vanished. This bank and the few families that own it control the economic systems of the world. They have at their helm, Master Mahan. Many of these controllers truly believe that Lucifer will be victorious and will conquer our **God**. He will not, but follow him if you will. You do have the right of choice.

Zion is even now being established. It will eventually lead the move to re-establish our Constitution, which will be more perfectly established than before. Our saved and reinforced Constitution will punish harshly, those who attempt to damage it. It will provide for perfect execution of the **Law of Liberty**. The whole of the Americas will become the Zion of our **God**. The **Law** will then go forth out of Zion, unto all the world. The thousand years of peace will be ushered in.

> The Russian Communism
> And the US Socialism
> Were only mirrors of each other
> They both set out to quell and smother
> The **Liberty** to which we cleave
> The freedom in which we believe
> But we will raise and hold on high
> An ensign which we'll proudly fly
> To show the world that crime is useless
> To teach the world of **God's** true justice
> To show the way to joy and peace
> And bring from suffering release
> The world will learn of law and order
> And **Liberty** will have no border
> Come now, let's do our Maker's work
> Let's not procrastinate or shirk
> We must now build a place of refuge
> Where true men can escape the deluge
> Of looting, rape and murder foul
> Of governments that hiss and growl
> And take from workmen all they make
> And claim it's for the worker's sake
> Yes! Come, help build Utopia
> Come help to save America

Out of poverty, equity; out of chaos, order. Having experienced lawlessness, many of us will be prepared to accept and help establish **Liberty Through Law**. The earth gives abundantly. In the new order, we won't give 80% plus of our production to the government. We won't be left with so little of the fruits of our labor that we can't survive without the money lenders. The 20% or so that's left to us after the government "rip off" won't have to be spent on necessities, priced crazily out of reason.

Greed won't cause physicians to charge many times the rate at which producers can earn the filthy lucre. Lawyers won't be needed in the coming society. Don't worry you guys, if you're among the few who have integrity, you'll have plenty to do in other fields. The rest of you won't want a place in a free society anyway. Money lenders won't exist. Usury (interest) is forbidden by

God's Law. Insurance magnates will be only a memory. Society won't pay ten times the pay back for protection they won't need anyway. The economic **Law of God** does not allow for people to lose all that they have over emergencies.

Yes, in the world to come, our efforts will net for us, enough and to some spare. We will, of course, gladly contribute that which we have beyond our own needs to care for those in need. We won't mind, because our security, our safety and confidence, will be assured through a perfectly equitable system.

God created and gave to man, this earth. He didn't hold a lottery to see who would win the greatest portions of it. Each and every citizen of earth, owns by **God given Right**, a piece of this planet. It was made for our use and we were told to subdue it. Where do governments or individuals get the idea that they can legitimately take control of the people's land? Why should we have to struggle for years of our lives to get control of a tiny plot on which to live? After we partially secure our tiny plot, why should we then pay taxes on it as a condition of our partial control of it?

When righteous laws are again in effect, citizens will be assigned their lot for their inheritance forever. It won't be taken from them for failure to pay taxes. Taxes on property are a tool of Lucifer, designed to give misery and insecurity to man. These taxes are illegal under **God's natural law**. Shame on you who are willing to be used as tools of evil in helping to impose these corrupt taxes.

In the new society you will have a legal right to lease out your property if you so choose. It will, by law though, revert back to you at the year of jubilee (every fifty years). You will not, therefore, be able to dispose of your family's rightful inheritance. Yes, everyone has a right to property and no one has a legitimate right to take it from them. Can you see any contrast between the right way and the way we do it?

In Zion, there will be no hunger. The old **law** required that the gleaning of the fields be left to the needy. They did the work of gleaning to sustain their own needs. In a more industrialized society, some deviations are necessary, but the basic principle will be the same. A method will be provided for all to obtain their needs. It won't be extracted from the producer though, to be given to the non-producer. This is unfair. Fairness and justice will be the rule in Zion.

We all will "sit under our own vine and fig tree." We all will have our own property as a "right." Upon our land we can produce our needs. If you decide to work for another, it will be by choice rather than need. If he offers enough pay to satisfy you, you may take employment. If, on the other hand, you don't like his terms, you can stay on your own, untaxed, owned outright land. You can produce what you will as an entrepreneur. It will be far easier to do your own thing when needs are not taxed and you're not forced to pay usury to obtain your requirements.

It is not an exaggeration to say that under our Babylonian System, the people retain for themselves, less than ten percent of the fruits of their labor. After paying multi-tier taxes on all your necessities, you then pay userous interest on your major needs. Many of you pay for insurance, which refunds less than ten percent of receipts.

A small portion of your taxes are used to educate your children. You have little to say about what they are taught. Of this much, you can rest assured, it is not conducive to creating honorable, decent citizens. In public education, your children are taught a lack of respect for authority. They are taught that they are expected to be promiscuous. In other words, they are taught whore-mongery and homosexuality. Also, they are taught that which has become the truth of our times, that parents have no rights over them (the children). In school, they learn that they have but to call in the authorities, if those housing, clothing, feeding them try to be more strict than they (the children) like. Make no mistake, these things are taught and become reality for many. The Lord said through the prophet Isaiah:[24] *As for my people, children are your oppressors and women rule over you.*

In Utopia, the rule will be; *Honor your father and your mother, that thy days may* be *long upon the earth which the **lord, thy God** giveth thee.*[25] Schools in the new world will quickly cease to exist if they attempt to interfere with a parent's authority.

Do you think wife beaters will be tolerated? Better for you to stay away if you are one of those cowards. The **Law of Liberty** provides public whippings for wife beaters. It is the only just penalty and it will be meted out. Thieves will repay in multiples, the value of their theft. This won't be a fine for government coffers. This will repay the victim and more to cover his inconvenience.

The people of Zion won't have to pay for a vast prison system. The "repayment with extra" system will soon convince most that crime in that system will **not pay**. Those who cannot well learn the lesson will simply be executed. The innocent will be protected. The criminal will not be tolerated. Criminals

---

[24] Isaiah 3:12
[25] Exodus 20:12

who cannot repay damage done, will, for a time, become producers of goods or services. This will be done under supervision of someone intelligent enough to make a profit from virtually free labor. The alternative to working to repay the wrong doing, will of course, be a **final solution**. The private businesses that avail themselves of the servitude of criminals will have the full support of the legal system, embodied in the *law of Liberty*.

The first deterrent to crime, of course, will be society's freedom to pursue happiness and to earn a decent living. The right to keep the fruits of their labor for themselves and their families will be paramount under **true and proper Law**. This will be the greatest crime deterrent of all. Second will be the legal requirement that society as a whole, be educated in their **Law**. **Correct Law**, is simple. Everyone can understand and see the logic in **law** that is designed strictly for society's good.

Think about it! If making a good living is not difficult, why break the **Law**? Why break the **Law** in a society wherein every individual knows he has a legal obligation to stop you? Yes, under **true Law**, simply allowing, knowingly, a crime to go unpunished, will be criminal. The penalty for a crime could be meted out to bystanders who fail to do their duty to prevent that crime, or bring to justice the perpetrator.

The bearing of false witness carries the same penalty as would be received by him being lied about. Yes, the imposition of correct and simple law will create a society wherein very little crime will exist. The **Law** will be so strict as to cause certain types of criminals (deviates) to curb their appetites. Because of this, the crimes blamed on genetic weakness, will naturally diminish with time. Self control, or restraint will be exercised more diligently in the face of penalties for **Law** breakers. Strength will breed strength and our race will improve.

> Our world will shrug and cast aside
> The rulers who are filled with pride
> We'll now take up on our own shoulder
> The duty to protect each other
> Our **Liberty** will be regained
> The criminal will be defamed
> And man will grow and soon regain
> The greatness that should in him reign
> In freedom, men will soon excel
> Its honor, good and right we'll sale
> To all with whom we ply our trade
> We'll show that we are truly made

Of sterner stuff than were the weaklings
That gave our freedom up to rantings
Of evil men from whose rank greed
We have decided to be freed

We're not ashamed to love our **God**, with all our heart and might
We're not afraid to wield the rod and champion the right
Within our borders, none but He, will be acclaimed as **Deity**
If you would worship otherwise, you'll find in us no sympathy
No other **Gods**, no other **Law**, for us can be accepted
On pain of death, we will defend this freedom we've recaptured
Because we are His children, because He loves us too
We can, but prove our love for Him, within the golden rule
You cannot wrong your fellow man while honoring your Maker
If you try this, your **God** will know you're nothing but a faker
We will not steal nor covet, nor take our neighbor's wife
For God decreed that all of us deserve a happy life
If you would bear false witness, tell lies about your brother,
Then you will rue the way you are for justice, you'll discover
Foul murder will soon be stamped out; we will not tolerate it
We will defend the innocent, from murderer or bandit
The punishment will fit the crime, kill and you'll be killed
In our fair land, all mankind will, with joy and peace, be filled
So you who seek the power to cheat, can live your lives of hell
While we who choose to keep **God's Law** will prosper and be well
Yes, you will be excluded from our society
Unless you're dedicated to help to keep men free
Come one, come all and join with us, to build our Zion fair
Let's join our **God** in **Liberty** and **Truth** and **Justice** there

The new society that is about to emerge will grow till it fills the whole earth.[26] Along with many others, Daniel foretold this occurrence with clarity. He described for the King of the Babylon of his day, the great Babylon of our day. Daniel likened different parts of the statue in the King's dream to various nations. Men have attempted ever since to decipher Daniel's interpretation.

The great question comes down to deciding which people are like unto the feet and toes made of iron and clay. The USA is described thusly, because we are the nation more than any other that has diversity of citizenry that cannot be mixed. Various metals can be blended together. Clay and iron will not alloy.

---

[26] Daniel 2:28-44

Our country is a melting pot of all the ethnicity of earth. We comprise every color or breed, together with every philosophy or religion known to man and a myriad of concepts about *justice*, administered under *Law*.

The author does not take a position as to right or wrong of diversity, except to the degree that his **God** has given clear and concise instructions or **Law**. Thou shalt have no other **Gods** before me means clearly, that we shall have no other **God's Law**. Call Him by whatever name you wish. Hate and harm your fellow man in his name and you prove yours to be a false **God**. A great man, a leader of men, said, *I don't care if a man worships a yellow dog, as long as that dog doesn't send that man to harm me and mine.*

Different peoples have different languages and call **Deity** by different names. The **God** of all peoples gave the *Law of Liberty* as the guide to freedom for all peoples. Diversity in acceptance of **God's** *Law of Liberty* is extensive in this land. We cannot be <u>alloyed</u> in this respect. Just one example: many believe in the right to life for the unborn, while more of us it seems, cannot accept that the unborn **have life** and cannot, therefore, admit that they should have **choice**.

The killing of our unborn is no different than the sacrificing of children that was practiced under the <u>*law*</u> of the imaginary <u>*god*</u>, Molech.[27] Those of you who practice, or even exonerate those who commit these murders, are following the *Law* of a false *God*. Like iron and clay, the <u>*laws*</u> of different <u>*gods*</u>, cannot blend harmoniously.

Another major impossible and improper attempt is the mixing of the seed. We see throughout our land, great contention over this subject, with much emotional discourse. The author lacks knowledge about teachings of prophets among peoples, other than Israel. He does see many Israelites, professing to accept their **biblical scriptures**, while propounding or extolling the virtues of interracial marriage. This has even become a political issue in this country. Speaking out against interracial marriage probably constitutes political suicide. Don't do it if you crave political power.

Isaiah certainly knew what he was talking about in lamenting; woe unto Israel in the last days, for calling good bad and bad good. The scriptures are very plain in forbidding Israel to inter-marry. Why will we deny it? If you do not profess belief in the Bible, you may make a weak argument. All Christians, Jews and many others, do **claim fealty** to **biblical law**. These are the vast majority among us. They should be given to understand that these **biblical laws** comply

---

[27] Leviticus 18:21

with **natural law** and are established strictly for our good.[28] These should be sufficient evidence for you as to your **God's** requirements pertaining to interracial marriage.

The author does not cringe when the terms: bigot, racist or prejudiced, are used on him. He believes strongly that all men should have equal opportunity and equal **justice**. He does not believe that anyone should demand **more** than these. If you chose to break **God's Law** under the guise of so-called anti-racism, the author cares nothing for your opinion. As reiterated throughout this work, those who will survive our times, emerging into a free society, will be those who will love and practice our **Creator's law**.

Yes, we are that society that is mixed with elements that cannot be joined to form compounds. We can no more blend than can iron and clay. We are that people which will be broken up by the Kingdom that will grow until it fills the whole earth. That Kingdom, **the literal Kingdom of God**, will have its birth here as this nation crumbles.

Zion will be established here in the Americas. We fit the description of Babylon, (18, Revelations). We also fit the description of the nation, likened by Daniel, to the mixture of clay and iron.[29] Daniel said that as this nation is broken up, the **Kingdom of God** will come forth, and from thence, will spread. The **Law** will go forth out of Zion to the whole earth. The **Kingdom of God** will go forth as a stone, that grows as it rolls, until it fills the whole earth.

If the Bible is false, if the prophets lied, then it is all so much garbage. The author believes biblical scripture to be true and fairly accurate in translation. For you who doubt or wonder, there have been many experiences in our day that prove the spirit world concept, as set forth in scriptures.

The book, ***Embraced By The Light***, by Betty J. Eadie, is a testimony by one of our contemporaries, who went to the "spirit world" and returned to tell us about it. Get the book and read it. You might be amazed. The author has known two people who testify to similar experiences. One was a Christian, the other a Jew. As stated, many similar cases have been documented. Dr. Melvin Morse, M.D., who wrote the "Forward" for Betty Eadie's book, claims to have interviewed many who have visited and returned from the spirit world.

---

[28] 1st Timothy 1:8
[29] Daniel 2:33-45

Those of you who really do believe the scriptures have not so much need of these testimonies as do the doubters. The doubters will only become believers, if they're willing to listen to their fellows who swear to these experiences and if they will look at the evidence of fulfilled prophecy. Of course, those who simply don't want to believe, never will. Those who wonder, can read and can pray. Anyone who does so, in sincerity, will accept the scriptures as divine. Anyone who understands that the scriptures are true, and will study them, will have to accept the truth of this warning.

God works in a mysterious way, His wonders to perform. The various organized religious groups put forth the idea that it is through them that salvation will come. The author puts it to you that the saving of **law abiding** citizens from **lawless** citizens or governments is the salvation mostly spoken of in scripture. It is put to you further that the churches are not preparing us for salvation. If we would be saved from the coming destructions, we must save ourselves by ingesting **God's Law** and keeping it. Those who do this and unite with others like themselves will find themselves to be the chosen seed. They will become the nucleus that will spearhead the establishment of Zion, the city of **God**.

The author will **not** foolishly **claim** that **no** church groups are preparing their congregations to accept **God's Law**. Some probably are, to some degree. More good is being done it seems by Rush Limbaugh, Michael Reagan, G. Gordon Liddy and others like them. These men are spreading "pearls of wisdom" far and wide. They stimulate us to think, and they show the American public that **all is not well**. These courageous men are shocking many out of complacency. They're stimulating many to take a second look at their belief that our government can do no wrong. Many among our citizenry are becoming more willing to analyze information for truth, because of these men. Whether they realize it or not, they're tools in the hands of **God**.

The author does not believe for one minute, that these great voices are infallibly right in all that they say. For instance, they will violently disagree with this call, this warning of death and destruction that has begun in our land.

These great conservative radio voices are helping us to see the choices that are before us. They expound on many of the injustices. They stimulate the people to scrutinize our condition. These pariah's are doing great good. If they were able to see and explain all, probably their effectiveness would diminish. They all set forth the belief that our problems, though serious, will be solved. These men can't see the fall, because they are personally very well off. This creates in them a desire for continuance of the system as we know it. Yes, they are wonderfully alert and able dispensers of truth. Yes, they very naturally fall just a little short of understanding the full import of our corruption.

The author truly believes these men to be, whether unwittingly or not, servants of our **Maker**. He knows that man is not capable of learning all, all at once. He gives us "line upon line, precept upon precept, here a little, there a little." In this manner, we can if we will, gradually assimilate sufficient knowledge and develop enough courage, strength and dedication, to be worthy of membership in a free society.

> It will take great courage, strength and wit, to keep yourself aloof
> When all around you join right in, to force on you their proof
> Or take from you, your precious wealth
> Steal your food and stalk in stealth
> They'll try to take your very life
> Your nation will be ripe with strife
> But, if you've learned your lessons well
> You'll stay far off from man-made hell
> And join with those who cherish peace
> To help the strong and true increase
> Yes, use your strength to pull away
> Refuse to jump into the fray
> For only thus, can honest men
> Deserve to live in freedom

If you are a thinker and an observer of your surroundings, you'll be sorely tempted to join one side or the other in the coming holocaust. The terrible dilemma before us now, is that for a time, it won't be a battle between good and bad. The evil one is marshalling his forces. He cannot obtain unity among his own. The great calamities we're facing have already begun. We will see simple magnification of this nation's rank criminality. The government, in attempting to fight crime and preserve itself, commits further crimes against its support base. The private sector fights back. Evil begets evil; crime begets crime. Our criminal elements will fight our criminal government until there is nothing left to fight for.

Who can say whether the government or the banks will fall first? Neither will exist much longer. When our green paper has no value, our transportation system will shut down. Who works without pay? Without transport, we all will travel only as fast as our legs can carry us. Cars won't run after the fuel depositories are emptied. Neither will grocery stores be stocked. How are **you** going to eat? If you have stored food, **can you defend it**?

Yes, these times have been predicted. Various religious groups have tried, from time to time, to pinpoint the supposed end of the world. The end of the world does not mean the extinction of mankind. It means the end of the world in chaotic condition; the end of **lawlessness**. It cannot be a smooth transition, because the **lawless** will not permit it to be so. In truth, "no man knoweth the day and the hour." We are not completely without intellect though, and signs were given that we might know that the time is near. The signs have been substantially completed.

The destruction by the sword has begun. The plagues have started to appear. The predicted increased intensity of destruction by the elements is very much in evidence. The only cleansing element not yet clearly in view is the promised fire. It will surely come and sooner than we wish.

Friends and loved ones often state that if their country falls, they'd as soon go down with it. One must wonder if they're considering only themselves, or do they reflect on the fact that their loved ones may perish with them? It is certain that as we ripen more fully in iniquity, the choices will become more evidently clear. It's all right to love your country and your way of life if they are reasonably healthy and conducive to clean living. The time is not far distant that it will be abundantly clear to all that our nation has sunk too deeply into the mire for salvation. Any who want peace and happiness, freedom for their families, must prepare to gather out.

The honest in heart, who will not take the sword up against their neighbor, will flee. *Pray that your flight will not be in the middle of the night, and in the dead of winter*. Pray that you will not be big with child, walking across the mountains in your bare feet. If you want to avoid these hardships, start looking for emissaries of Zion who can guide you there. The author does not claim to know the mind of **God**. Scripture is plain though, and Zion will be established. Israel will be warned and will be gathered.

In Zion, men will not work all the day, all the week, for all the year, barely earning their family's needs. Neither will mothers have to leave their children to others in order to help feed the whole world while keeping a few left over scraps for their own. That which we produce will mostly be ours to keep. More of our time will also be our own. You won't have to worry most of the time about your future ability to support your family. Men will not, in droves, break under the unnatural pressures and go berserk, committing unspeakable atrocities.

Inflation will be unknown in Zion. Children will grow up without an inkling of such stupidity as constantly increasing costs. A study will be made by knowledgeable people to determine the values of commodities. The values will be related to each other on a basis of the effort needed to produce, store, transport and distribute them to consumers. If, for instance, a bushel of wheat takes twice as much effort to produce and get to market as does the same quantity of corn, the wheat will accordingly be worth twice as much as the corn.

The free enterprise system will, of course, allow for bargaining. Basic values though, will be established on the basis of cost. Money will have no value, except as a convenient medium of exchange. Money won't be a rentable commodity. Fluctuating values of money will not control our economy, nor even affect it. We will not have priests of Master Mahan telling the people that interest is being raised to fight inflation, the interest to begin with being the most basic cause of inflation. Government will not have the ability to destroy its own citizenry, taking from citizens to feed itself, its greed, power mongery and false aggrandizement.

Come! Join with us who cherish **freedom**, come help us to regain it
Let us go forth with might and zeal to overcome the culprit
We will take back that which we've lost, through our complacency
And we'll be **free**, because we'll choose, the **Law of Liberty**
Don't go forth to battle, unless you're called by **God**
For if you do, your sure reward is underneath the sod
Just hold you back and keep the peace, it's hard, but you can do it
If you will heed this warning voice, you'll surely win the gambit
Yes, let the evil forces just wipe themselves clear out
Then you'll be left and you and yours can then raise **freedom's shout**

Oh, we must keep ourselves aloof
We must not join the battle
It's only through staunch abstinence
That we can prove our metal
Gird up your loins
My stalwart ones
Be strong, true, and valiant, and show that you are worth
A place among the truly **free** that **God** is calling forth

Don't you go out and get involved in criminality
This is truly not the way to build a place that's **free**
It will be harder to abstain from entering the fight
When you can see on every hand, the tearing down of right
We must hold out and strive for peace, if ever more will we

Qualify to dwell within the **land of Liberty**
The "helter skelter" groups are taking up the fight
Beat the urge to join with them; resist with all your might
Because if you join in, you'll just become one more
To fight the losing battle, against the gluttonous whore
Yes! She'll go down, she cannot stand, against the mighty throng
But, so will those who fight her, for their reasons too are wrong
The only ones who will survive the holocaust that's coming
Are those who'll keep themselves away and seek the glorious morning
When Israel will be gathered and Zion will be here
And peace and love and **freedom** will take away all fear
Yes! Let them hiss and piss and moan and kill each other dead
While we will glory and rejoice, for Zion will be led
By emissaries of our **God**, who surely will be heard
And all within our land will know, our **Law** is our **God's word**

The poet cannot stress too much, the need for abstenation
You must not join the battle's fray, do show propitiation
Refrain from taking sides among the devilish demons
Or you will find yourself among the suffering and dead ones

Only a couple of years or so ago, the author began to write down some thoughts. He couldn't help but see the acceleration on a graduated scale, of criminality, throughout our nation. It was evident then that the previous thirty five years had brought almost unbelievable advances into evil, self destructive practices. A few essays were written, really as musings at first, without much thought to publishing them.

Over the last couple of years, immorality and blatant criminality have increased at an even faster rate it seems, than ever before. If we are allowed to continue, the result will probably be the extinction of the human race upon this earth. It has happened before; it is easy to see the possibility of this accomplishment once more. **God** vowed, though, to take a hand and to lead out of the chaos, those who will agree to **Liberty for all**.

God can't wait much longer or there will be nothing left for him to salvage. He has, therefore, begun the work to save us from ourselves. His spirit is intensifying to reach the ones who'll make a little effort. Here and there, from different walks of life, Israelites are waking up. They're beginning to realize that our only salvation will come from the practicing of the **Law of Liberty**. The Lord **God,** through the prophet Jeremiah said: *Behold, the days come, saith the Lord, that I will make a new covenant with the house of Israel, and with the* *house of Juda: Not according to the covenant that I made with their fathers in the day that I took them by the hand to bring them out of the land of Egypt; which covenant they brake, although I was an husband to them, saith the Lord: But this shall be the covenant that I will make with the house of Israel; After those days, saith the Lord, I will put my law in their inward parts, and write it in their hearts; and will be their God, and they shall be my people.*[30]

While this is a promise made by our **Creator**, it still requires our acceptance. The covenant cannot be completed until Israel receives, and is willing to put it into practice. It will be done, of course. The time is now, not some distant, future expectation. The destruction and the gathering have begun. The sooner you can join in, the easier you will find the transition. The longer you wait, the greater the chance of hardships along the way.

---

[30] Jeremiah 31:31-33

CHAPTER 8

The majority of our countrymen just don't want to hear doom and gloom about our home land. It's not pleasant to dwell on, but if we don't face the truth, what chance have we of dealing with it? Unless you are hoary with age, you have difficulty relating correctly to the economic condition of your people. If you put a frog into slightly warm water, then heat it slowly to the boiling point, the frog doesn't know what hits him. Drop a frog into hot water and he'll jump out or writhe and squirm in his death throes. We are like the frog. Our subjugation has come upon us so gradually that it seems almost natural.

The older among us know how much more their efforts netted for themselves in earlier years. The "Great American Dream" the politicians like to spout off about, used to be possible. Comparing the spending power of today's devalued dollar to the dollar of fifty years ago cannot begin to convey the difference. For accurate comparison, one must relate the effort needed then, to the effort needed now, for acquisition of one's needs.

Of course knowledge has been amassed. Assembly line production methods and vastly improved materials have been developed. These things though, should have lightened our burdens instead of adding to them. More modern conveniences are available to us today because of technology. The efforts that we must expend though, and the stress we're under to keep up, are terribly excessive. Many of our fellows are breaking under the strain.

You can look down on the homeless, if you will. They now number into the millions. The prisoners we have behind bars are as much a result of our idiotic system as are the homeless. They, or the families that raised them, couldn't cut it in our inequitable economy. The criminals who are not imprisoned are, of course, a large multiple of those in captivity. Welfare and food stamp recipients again prove the inadequacy of our ways.

Yes, you can look down on, or sneer at these beleaguered dregs of our society. When doing so, you exercise the false pride that goeth before the fall. There is nothing in this world to make you different from them but luck. Your good fortune may have been environmental opportunity or simply genetic. No one can say, though, what kind of life different circumstances might have brought.

It's easy to say that the homeless young man, by choice, just gave up. When he has a wife and small children, what do you say about them? If you are prospering, how wonderful for you. You probably work hard to earn your prosperity. You probably have reasonable intelligence. If so, you cannot deny that your efforts are unalterably tied to our way of life as a society. If you are a house painter, your peers must prosper somewhat or they can't hire you. You might be a mechanic, a waitress or whatever. There is very little that one can do towards acquisition of needs that is not tied to the needs of others.

"Rich man, poor man, beggar man, thief
Doctor, lawyer, merchant chief"
Banker, builder, boiler maker
Actor, singer, tassel shaker
We all must sell our wares somewhere
Those who can't will seek welfare
And then their peers will sneer and jeer
Making them wish they weren't here
Society looks down on those who don't do well
And many of their children live a life of hell
They feel that they're not good enough
They know that they're considered rough
Sure, they react in consternation
To sneering and humiliation
And sure you say, It's their own fault
Because their father couldn't halt
Inflation, interest, unemployment
Or persecution for enjoyment
Of some rank government official
Whose aim in life is never moral
Who glories in his place of power
Over some poor slob that's weak or lower
And therefore subject to dominion
And to the "great one's" subjugation
You are asked to please consider
That in this world of sweet and bitter
We all can't always be successful
We all can't always keep the horn full
In a system like our own
Where love and charity have flown
To be replaced with greed for money
We all cannot have milk and honey
Some succeed, while others fall
Our code does not make room for all
Because we feed upon each other

151

> The lofty watch the lowly smother
> The high and mighty are only so
> Compared to those who've been brought low

A period of great mercy must be granted to mankind in simple justice. Our **Law Maker**, our **God**, has probably had mixed emotions about allowing this society so much latitude. By original agreement, He has had to let us go until it is certain that we will nevermore allow freedom for each other. Being our Father, it must grieve Him deeply to watch our treatment of our brothers and sisters. Only those of you who are fathers or mothers can begin to understand this.

Do you have children and love them? How do you feel when your children injure one another? Do you love them enough to establish fair rules for their treatment of each other? If you don't love your children, you may not care if one gains more wealth than the others by stealing from and subjugating them. If you do love them, though, you'll not allow this, especially if you first provided them with productive properties for the use of all.

A chicken farmer named Joseph Val raised more than chickens. Farmers know all about the birds and the bees. Joe was no exception. He raised some lovely daughters and several stalwart sons. Joe loved his children and wanted for them, nothing but the best. He knew that they could make a good living at farming, if left alone by the government. Joe knew though, that his children would not all be happy in his chosen profession. Against his better judgement, he succumbed to his wife's wheedling, sending his children off to public school.

The oldest boy, Steven, had already flown the coop. He'd gone off to law school, where because of his brilliance and perseverance, he was, ultimately, the youngest ever to graduate from Yale. Steve's success helped to defray Joe's suspicion of contemporary educators.

The younger children, attended the same B school, which included elementary and junior high school grades. The school was in the city, so the children had a long walk in the brisk early morning. They arose very early in order to finish their chores and arrive to class on time. The long walk, or run, to and from school is not so important to the narrative as the fact that they were outsiders. They were farmers, from out in the boondocks. School kids are cliquish. City kids often find pleasure in belittling and harassing outsiders. Farm kids in a city school invariably become the brunt of jokes and degradation.

The little girls, Cassandra and Melissa, didn't understand. When teased, they became belligerent and gave back as good as they got. This could not be tolerated by the united block of city kids. Sticks and stones began to fly. The girls were outnumbered. Ben and Paul came to their aid, and got for their efforts, bloodied noses, black eyes, the normal bruises one would expect and more. When little kids scrap with bigger kids and are outnumbered, the result is predictable. They were soundly beaten.

David and Logan, the oldest of Joe's children attending the Denver suburb school, were fine looking youths. At twelve and fourteen years old, these farm boys were straight and tall and strong. They were handsome, light skinned, dark haired boys. Their facial features were finely cut, chisel sharp, but delicate like their mothers. The girls fell all over them. They were popular with the guys too, because of their strength and athletic ability. Running three miles to and from school was good training for track and other sports.

The joshing that David and Logan received for their "farm boy" background was just good natured fun. Of course they were as big as any in the school and just didn't look bullyable. They enjoyed their popularity, and in fact, one might say they reveled in it.

Joe is one of those people who can be infuriating in an argument or disagreement. He's just damned bullheaded. He won't change his mind or opinion simply because you see things differently. You have to present him with good logic if you want him to consider your point. Genetics being what they are, Joe passed his stubbornness on to his children.

Ben and Paul could have saved themselves some bruises by simply crying uncle. The older boys felt they had to prove themselves the masters. They demanded subservience to the extent of apologies for being dumb farmers. They couldn't extract this admission. It was an impasse. These guys had their pride and couldn't stop in front of the audience without the demanded confession.

Poor Paul and Ben got more of a beating than usually takes place when youths fight. They were hurt badly enough that they'd never again hang around the schoolyard after school. Fat and split lips, bloody noses, black eyes and skinned knuckles, go with scrapping kids. Paul got a broken nose though, and Ben a cracked rib. Joe couldn't quite accept this for eight and ten year old boys.

David and Logan had finally stepped in to stop the lopsided fight. They had anguished from the start, but their popularity was important to them. They hurt at their little brothers' plight, but hated so to chance the ire of their admirers.

153

They surely wished they'd been quicker to protect their own, though, when contemplating the coming meeting with their father. That part of it didn't cross their minds in the excitement in the school yard. They had three long miles in which to anticipate the very just retribution that they knew was their due upon dad's inspection of their brothers. The sisters had been roughed a little too and didn't appear to be promising witnesses for defense of the older boys.

Well, Joe didn't disappoint his children. He did not fly off the handle, but meticulously questioned each participant of the incident. The older boys didn't lie. They were ashamed, but they told the truth. They hated to chance being on outs with their peers, but knew they'd paid too high a price for acceptance.

Now Joe came from the old school. Of course, he'd read Dr. Spock and listened to opinions from the do-gooders who've raised our present nation of juvenile delinquents. He was a wise man though, and understood that you don't show love by allowing or training your children to become criminals. Joe was a student of the **Good Book**. He understood that under the *Law of Liberty*, one cannot stand by and watch crime, doing nothing to protect the innocent. This **Law** demands that we defend not only ourselves, but our neighbors also.

What penalty would you expect Joe, a student of scripture, to find to be fair? He determined that he who refuses to defend his neighbor is guilty as though he'd been the perpetrator of the crime. He was further convinced that the punishment should fit the crime. Like the biblical Law concerning wife beating; give a beating, get a beating. The boys followed instructions, cutting and bringing to Joe, willow branches to meet his specifications. This meant large enough to stand up to the strain, yet small and pliable enough to sting through their britches without excessive skin damage.

The damage to the younger boys was considerable. Joe felt terrible, inside he was torn to pieces, but was wise enough to know that his beloved children needed this lesson. He knew that only in youth is character molded. Joe knew that his children could not grow up to be decent, honorable, law abiding citizens without proper guidance. He knew that they'd infringed on natural law and that if they went un-punished, they'd know they could get away with wrong doing. These boys were feeling pretty badly about themselves, just then. Their shame, in fact, went deep. They actually relished the punishment that would make their repentence complete. Neither were the younger boys very happy with them. They would not have believed their heroes would allow them to be bullied. That hurt as much as the physical pain. It's funny about emotion. Those kids hurt and were mad at their brothers. For all of that, they wouldn't have had the heart to administer justice. Had Ben and Paul been required to wield the switch, they couldn't have done it. They would have forgiven David and Logan. Under that condition, though, their hero worship would have greatly diminished. They would not, thereafter, have had quite as much love and respect for their brothers.

Yes, administering judgement for infraction of statutes is usually difficult. Raising children to be good and law abiding citizens, cannot be done without some heart rending circumstances. Joe was strong enough and he loved his children sufficiently. He had another very rare and wonderful circumstance to aid him with this very difficult task. Joe had a wife who also understood that training children properly would bring them (the children) happier, more productive, more complete lives, for all their lives.

Yes, Joe suffered, but he did gird up his loins (bolster up his courage) and did wield the rod and did welt the back sides of his beautiful, loving sons. With great courage, he whacked away until each respectively cried out that it was enough. The wife of course, hid away, sobbing her eyes out. Joe cried inside for days. The boys, though, were over it by the next day and were proud of their dad's spanking ability. In later years they would often brag about their fathers firmness with them.

Had these young men gone unpunished, they'd have suffered pangs of guilt for as long as their memories would sustain them. Internally, they would have suffered greatly and long. This kind of suffering, though, usually does not strongly effect actions. They might have again acted in like manner. Breaking the law once makes a criminal of the perpetrator. Repetitive law breaking can become a habit almost impossible to break. Sure, swift punishment, removes guilt, leaving innocence in its wake.

Joe's younger children were able immediately to forgive completely, their brothers, seeing them properly punished. Of course, their hearts swelled with pride and love, watching their father meet out justice on their behalf. For some, just watching the execution of judgement, can be sufficient deterrent to criminal behavior. Others may need to feel the rod. It is damn sure that no one ever respects law and order without some respect building experiences in youth.

The older boys also felt good about themselves again. They'd paid the price and did not therefore have to carry around the guilt and shame. Do you think they loved their father less? If so, they were good actors, because they showed more **respect** and **affection** for some time after their spanking.

The famous spanking took place on a Tuesday. The boys dressed for gym on Wednesday. Marks from the switching were still visible on their upper thighs and buttocks. Oh, Oh! Here was evidence of brutality. Here was unquestionable child abuse. The track coach heard talk among the boys. He took a look for himself and was incensed. How dare this chicken farmer abuse these poor little boys.

When the social worker came, David and Logan were appalled. They told everyone that would listen that they were not abused, that spankings at their house were rare and only when deserved. You can imagine how much attention was paid to their pleas. We live in a world where powerful administrators were raised by mothers who hadn't the fortitude nor the inclination to raise children to understand right from wrong. How could it be otherwise in a world like ours. Women have so little pride and so little love for their progeny that they no longer attempt to guarantee honorable birth and strong family government to their prospective young.

By the millions, single, young girls lay on their backs for irresponsible men, (young and old). If they allow the resulting offspring to live, a very large number of them are raised with no training as to right and wrong. These grow up and become a part of the whole of us. A good many of the contributing members of today's society simply have very little understanding about proper Law. **God** bless the females. They're lovely, they can give youth the love and nurturing they need, but they cannot change their nature. They cannot instill respect for authority in their children. Of course there are rare exceptions, but the vast majority of people raised by single parents lack some of the needed ingredients of rearing to make them into well-rounded, productive citizens.

Can a leopard change its spots? Can stink weed smell like roses? Remember the expression, "he thinks his doesn't smell?" It does though. All the love and desire in the world cannot teach a boy that his mother is an authority figure to be feared. When he's small and being spanked, he's cogniting on the fact that someday he'll be bigger and stronger than she is. A woman who is willing to spend all her time and energy with her children may win enough love from them and some respect so that they may develop into good citizens. For the most part, though, the women who are willing to have illicit relationships are too self-centered to give all their efforts to their progeny.

Just wanting one's children to become honorable adults, respectful of one another's rights, doesn't do it. Mostly we become what we're trained to become. Our government today is riddled with these untrained dregs, who rail about curbing crime with more jails and more policemen. **God** save the Queen, He can't save the people. Only people can raise children to either respect each other's rights, or not to. If it's not instilled in youth, it never will be. All the corrupt politicians and policemen in the world cannot, even through force, instill even a minute amount of respect in those who've been raised without it.

Only that portion of our society who are raised within units of strong family government, have even a small chance of qualifying as honest, law abiding citizens. Of these, all will not make it. Teach perfect truth, then send your kids to school to be taught how stupid your "victorian" views are. You can't send them off to be taught and expect them to ignore those teachings. You can only expect a small portion of your teachings to be honored.

Well, Joe Val learned how idiotic our system has become. Joe administered justice within his governing jurisdiction. He found that his government no longer backs up his authority as a father. He did a couple of days behind bars before his family could raise the bail money. The boys later claimed to have suffered much more from the humiliation of being required to bare their arses to police photographers, than from the whipping. Neither were they pleased at having the jurors inspect photos of their behinds. The television was the worse part. We'll leave to your imagination, the enhancement done by the sadistic news reporters.

David and Logan learned respect for their father from their father. They were not so stupid as to maintain a high opinion of the regulatory agencies that meddled with their family. Neither did they gain a high regard for the aiding and abetting police officers, who treated him as a common criminal.

Joe was subjected to authority of typical bureaucratic dumb heads. He was charged with brutalizing his children. He was fortunate to have a brilliant son for a lawyer. Steven did a good job, but he was young and inexperienced. He didn't win a not guilty verdict, but the penalty might have been much more severe without his supreme effort.

Most jurors just *know* that the government *won't* bring charges without good cause. Thank heaven for the small percentage of today's citizenry that has had a decent raising. A couple of the jurors couldn't find it in their hearts to convict Joe for having tried to teach his children to be good.

The jury argued and kibitzed and harangued for days. Finally, as compromise, the two hold outs agreed that if sentencing would be limited to fines, they'd join the crowd to convict. Well, at least the brutalized children would still have a bread winner. The farm of course had to be sold. At auction it brought about half it's value. Full price would almost have paid the fine levied by the old bitch of a "judge" who'd never had children, but fancied herself, "defender of the weak."

The older boys agreed to help pay off the loan which was arranged to cover the balance of the fine to keep dad out of jail. This meant after school work and of course, no chance for college. At least the walk home after school or work would be easier. The slums they had to move into were not far from school. The farm had only been worth about a Quarter of a Million of today's inflated Dollars. Not much of a start when divided between seven inheritors. It would have helped, though, when Joe's health failed due exclusively to the pressures (Stress) he suffered at the hands of his *glorious* government.

Well, don't you worry. Our socialistic system has developed into one which provides for all. In government funded schools your children will be taught how fortunate they are to be a part of our glory. There still are a few farms around the country. Those on government payrolls (dole) can continue for awhile at least. Don't forget that they have many other methods of extracting the resources of the producers. We probably have a few more years before all production is halted in our country. Surely then, the countries throughout the world whose heads we've made rich, *will come to our aid*. Don't you think so?

Of course, the parable of Joe Val is only that, a parable. If your eyes are open, if you can see and hear, you know that more outrageous true stories unfold very regularly, all over this land. The efforts of the capable are constantly usurped by the power mongers. "The Butt Pirates" cannot survive by any other means. In their arrogance, they cannot see beyond their noses. Their cannibalism will cease with their starvation, after they completely consume their supporters. Why can't they see this?

CHAPTER 9

In Zion, government will be "Patriarchal" period. Fathers will be in charge of the children that they raise and support. We will have judges, but they won't be political appointees, nor will they be lawyers. All in Zion will learn the very simple **Law of Liberty**. Judges will be selected from among those of you who demonstrate wisdom, morality and humanitarianism. Government will be a loose confederation of families with the fathers at the head. A **King** will eventually be appointed by the father of us all. The **King** will act the part of a grand patriarch like Abraham, Moses, Christ, or the expected Messiah. **The Law of the Fathers** will protect instead of persecuting and bleeding us.

God's Law requires that all citizens learn the **Law** and **participate** in the execution thereof. Citizens are required under this **Law** to **stop** crime wherever they see it. We will have **no need** of police forces. **We all will defend us all instead of us all paying our all for someone else to persecute in the guise of protecting us.**

Isaiah's description of our times; *good will be called bad and bad will be called good*, is very clear in relationship to our law enforcement agencies. These **Gestapos** stress very strongly that we have no business taking justice into our own hands. It is, according to them, their jurisdiction. They couldn't be more wrong. **Responsibility for justice, the right to execute the same, rests one hundred percent upon the shoulders of the people.**

Out of laziness and cowardice we hire the power hungry to take on our responsibility. They love it. They, of course, usurp all we allow and more of diabolical authority over us. They arm themselves and do their best to disarm us, who pay them salaries to oppress us. Once enough **Israelitish freedom lovers** have gathered, Zion will be born in strength and power. The police force in Zion will be her citizens; **all of them**. Infringe on their rights and your neighbors will stop you. Along with acceptance of this responsibility comes the saving of your resources that otherwise would be paid to police forces.

As Israel gathers together, withdrawing herself from our **lopsided** society, Babylon will be destroying herself. This message will reach whom it reaches. Some few of you who read this will exercise the key for discernment of truth. The same message will be spread in many ways. It is filtered throughout Holy Writ. Most will probably have to see it unfold before their eyes and still will have great difficulty turning loose of Babylonian ways. Of course, as our evil system progresses, the honest in heart will be unable to keep their heads buried.

So much about our system was good, even inspired by **God**, that we cannot help but grieve at its passing. Master Mahan has gained control though, and rules the hearts and minds of most of our compatriots. That which was sweet has turned sour. Our pleasant indulgences have become bitter. Don't be like **Lot's wife** who so hated leaving Sodom that she couldn't qualify for the salvation that was offered her. Yes, we once had a semblance of freedom. It is gone though, and will not return without the cleansing promised by **God**.

Watch for emissaries from Zion, the elders of Israel, and join with them. Mingle with the children of Abraham who will come down out of the north countries to claim their birthright. He will gather Israel as a hen gathereth her chicks[31] and he will be their **God** and they will be his people.[32]

A treatises is included hereafter, which humbled the author and which he hopes will somehow be disseminated to all his people. This treatise is anonymous. It is so wonderfully written that the author feels greatly blessed to have discovered it. Whoever wrote this article must have been a prophet of **God**.

<u>The Coming Crises, and How to Meet it</u>

A great and awful crisis is at hand-such a crisis was never known before since the foundation of the world. All nations are looking through the misty future, in order to descry, if possible, what is about to happen...

But says the reader, I would like to know of what this crisis is to consist! Who are the contesting parties? Well, reader, if you will be patient and honest-hearted, praying withal, with unceasing diligence and thanksgiving to God, you shall have the keys of such knowledge as all the sectarian priests of Christendom are by no means able to reveal, because they are only revealed to God's servents, the Prophets...

Perhaps you will be disappointed, if I tell you that the time is coming, and now is, when not only God, the highest of all, shall be revealed in spirit and in mighty power, but the Devil or Satan also, will be revealed in signs and wonders, and in mighty deeds! This reader, is the great key to all the marvelous events that are to transpire shortly upon the earth...

Now just stop right here, and pause and mark emphatically this key. Then you and I will proceed to unlock the mysteries and to prepare ourselves to the

---

[31] Jeremiah 16:15, 23:8 & Matthew 23:37
[32] Jeremiah 32: 37-38

battle. For there will be no neutrals in the approaching controversy. I say again that God the Highest of all will make bare His arm in the eyes of all nations. And the heavens even will be rent and His power will be felt by all nations. But this is not all, Satan, will also be revealed. He has made some manifestations of his power in different periods of the world, but never before has there been an array of numbers on his side, never before such consolidation of armies and rulers, never befor has there been such an imposing and overwhelming exhibition of miracles as Satan will shortly make manifest. Don't suppose for a moment, that I am uttering dark sayings or speaking unadvisedly upon speculation or the strength of mere human opinion. Don't tell me about Popes and Prelates sitting in the temple of God as God. One far greater than any Pope or Prelate is soon to be revealed, and he will claim to be worshipped as God. Now remember, that it is no modern wicked man that is going to claim divine honors. No, it is that old serpent, the Devil. He it is that will head the opposition against God and his Christ. And he, the son of perdition it is, that will be allowed a much longer chain than heretofore. And such will be the greatness of his power, that it will seem to many that he is entirely loose. He will be so far unshackled and unchained that his power will deceive all nations, even the world. And the elect will barely escape the power of his sorceries, Enchantments, and miracles! And even God, Himself the true God, will contribute to put means and instruments in his way and at hand for his use, so that he can have a full trial of his strength and cunning, with all deceivableness of unrighteousness in them that perish...

It is not to be expected that Satan will carry on his great warfare against Crist and his Saints, by means of any one religion exclusively. It is not the Papal or protestant religion alone that you have need to fear. But the great and abominable Church which you should expect to encounter is Anti-Christ, whether it is a civil or religious power. But the most formidable power that will be arrayed against Christ and His Saints in the last days, <u>will consist in the revelations of Satan</u>. These revelations of Satan will come through every medium and channel by which the cunning and power of Satan can be brought. It is a great mistake to suppose that Satan is altogether a religious personage. No, far from this. He is a politician, a philosopher, and erudite scholar, a linguist, a metaphysician, a military commander, a prince, a god, a necromancer, and enchanter, a diviner, a magician, a sorcerer , a prophet, and (if it were not railing) a clergyman and liar from the beginning. With these universal endowments, he has never hitherto made a full and grand exhibition of himself, as it remains for him to do. But the Lord, who gave him an opportunity to try his battery upon good old Job, is fully designing to give him sufficient apparatus to deceive all nations that love not the truth, and have pleasure in unrighteousness. His signs and tokens are as ancient as the apostacy of Cain, and as varied as will suit the secret designs of all ages. Through him men learn to become "observers

161

of times and seasons", with great skill and astonishing accuracy. He presides over the arts of astrology, clairvoyance, mesmerism, electro-biology, and all auguries and divinations. Being Prince of the power of the air, he understands aeronautics and steam navigation, and he can compose and combine the various elements through the cooperation of them that believe in him, with far more than human skill. Now don't doubt what I say concerning this matter, but rather read the history of his skillful exploits and his mighty power, as they are recorded in the Old and New Testaments. Take a Bible and Concordance, (if you have any faith in the Bible, left, in an age when the Bible is perverted beyond all other books) and read attentively for yourselves and you will learn that I am telling you the truth...

Now there is a greater destruction coming upon the wicked nations of the earth, than was even experienced by Pharaoh at the Red Sea. But before that destruction can be made manifest, men's hearts will be hardened, and wickedness will rise to a more overwhelming hight than many bye-gone generations have been allowed to witness. God, through His Prophet, will roar out of Zion, His voice will be heard in spite of all the confusion and indignant opposition from many nations. _After the testimony of his servants has been proclaimed to all nations, as a witness, then shall the scene of the end come. And great shall be that scene. The Devil in the last stage of desperation, will take such a pre-eminent lead in literature, politics, philosophy and religion: in wars, famines, pestilences, earthquakes, thunderings and lightnings, setting cities in conflagration, etc., that mighty kings and powerful nations will be constrained to fall down and worship him. And they will marvel at his great power, and wonder after him with great astonishment. For his signs and wonders will be among all nations._ Men will be raised for the express purpose of furthering the designs and marvelous works of the devil. Every description of curious and mysterious arts that penetrate beyond the common pale of human sagacity and wisdom, will be studied and practiced beyond what has been known by mere mortals. The great capabilities of the elements of fire earth and water, will be brought into requisition by cunning men under the superior cunning of the prince and god of this world and inflated with the knowledge of these wonderful arts and powers, men will become boasters, heady, high-minded, proud and despisers of that which is good...

But the God who is above all, and over all, and who ruleth in the armies of heaven, and amongst the inhabitants of the earth, will not be a silent observer of such spiritual wickedness in high places, and among the rulers of the darkness of this world. For the master spirits of wickedness of all ages, of worlds visible and invisible, will be arrayed in the rebellious ranks before the closing scene shall transpire. Now just at this time , God will come out of his hiding place and vex the nations in His hot displeasure. By the mouth of His Prophet, He will rebuke strong nations afar off, notwithstanding their strong armies, great miracles, and cunning arts...

His servant, the Prophet in Zion will have a marvelous boldness to rebuke them, and to lay down before them in plainness and inflexible firmness, the law of the Lord. As Moses laid down the law of Pharaoh, and continued to multiply evils and judgement until he made an utter end of Pharaoh and the Egyptians, even so will the living God prescribe the line of conduct to be pursued, and the penalties of violation, to great and mighty nations, until they rally around the ensign established upon the mountains, and go up to the house of the God of Jacob to learn His ways, or are utterly overwhelmed in keen anguish and ruin...

Ye perhaps marvel that the great men and governors of over one hundred and twenty-seven provinces in ancient Babylon, with a brave monarch at their head, should have been such firm believers in the astrologers, magicians, and interpreters of dreams in their days! But marvel not, for when the greater power of the like class of persons under the direction of Satan, shall be brought to bear in your own day, the delusions will be so much stronger, that Princes, Presidents, Governors, and chief Captains, will be constrained to bow to it. Their credulity will be taxed beyond the power of resistance. The workers of these mysterious and supernatural causes that will challenge and defy disputation...

The senses and judgement of men cannot withstand such imperative facts as will arrest their observation. For it cannot withstand such imperative facts of the ingredients of these mysterious and wonderful arts will give them an irresistible strength of conviction to those who are unenlightened by the spirit of God. And so far as facts and truth are mingled, it must also be acknowledged that God, the true and living Sovereign of heaven and earth, will contribute to produce the delusion. He has said that "He will send them strong delusions that they might believe a lie." He gives his reason and apology for acting after this strange manner-because knowing the truth, they do not love it unadulterated...

Knowing God, they do not choose to glorify Him as God. Therefore, their foolish hearts become darkened, and God suffers Satan to compound and mix up truth and error in such proportions as to be captivating and strongly delusive. As a snare, this composition will be ingeniously mixed and administered to all nations by skillful and practiced hands.

And who shall be able to withstand? Do you think that your great sagacity and the compass of your profound philosophical turn of mind will enable you to detect the error and delusion of these arts? Oh, man, this is a vain hope. Your mind will not be competent to detect the delusion. God himself will allow Satan *to ply your scrutinizing eye with powers and sophistications far beyond your capacity to detect, Do you say then, I will stand aloof from investigation. I will shun all acquaintance with these mysterious workings, In order that I may not be carried away with their delusive influence. Vain hope. Oh, man, you cannot be neutral, You must choose your side and put on your arms...*

    Those who do not come to the help of the Lord in the day of battle, will be sorely cursed. The captive Hebrew, Daniel stood up boldly against all the governors and whole realm of Babylon with their monarch at their head. But Daniel readily acknowledged that it was not for any wisdom in him, above other men, that he could surpass the astrologers and magicians. But holding intercourse with the God of heaven, he became endowed with a supernatural delusion, Thereby he escaped the snare that entwined around the great statesmen and governors of the immense empire of Babylon. <u>Thereby those who take refuge in the name of the Lord, and in immediate revelation from heaven, will be safe, and no others.</u> He that is not for God and the principle of immediate revelation, will inevitably be ensnared, overcome and destroyed. Because he that is not for Him is against Him. No man in any age was ever for God, or even a friend of God, that did not hold intercourse with Him personally, and receive for himself the revelation, by which Peter knew Jesus Christ, and this is the only basis upon which any man can escape the strong delusion which God will send among the nations, through Satan and his mediums and coadjutors. Reader, if you live long, you will be compelled to take side with God or Satan. Satan was allowed to try a compulsory process upon as good a man as Job. The whirlwind and tempestuous process with disease and death, were put into Satan's hands that he might compel Job to abandon his integrity. Had not Job possessed the key of revelation from God, he would have been compelled to have made peace with Satan, and forsaken the Lord. His wife urged him to do so - says she, "Curse God and die;" or, in other words, take the side of Satan against God. Now, reader, if you have ships of precious merchandise floating at sea, the time is fast coming when Satan will destroy those ships, unless you bow down to his power and become a co-operator with him. And if you do bow down to him, to work wickedness and say, no eye seeth me - then God will destroy those ships and you too, and peradventure He will destroy your family also, and make a clean end of you, and blot out your name under heaven. Your beautiful mansion and flourishing family will have to be consecrated to God or to Satan, whichever you may choose. The controversy is begun and the war will never end till the victory is complete and universal, and there shall not be found so much as a dog to move his tongue against the Lord, and the immediate revelations of His will... For the time has come that God will write His law upon every man's heart that will receive it, not with ink, but with the Spirit of the Living God. And against him *that hath this law, the gates of hell never have prevailed and never will prevail. Heaven and earth shall not be made to succumb to wicked men or devils...*

The heavens have been shaken once when angels rebelled and they are destined to another shaking even with the earth. Do you say you don't need any more revelation from God? Then the Devil will be allowed to give you some which you don't need. And by the time that he has revealed himself to you, and buffetted you, and trained you under his rigorous discipline to fight in this awful crisis against the heavens, peradventure you will not then feel so rich and increased in good, but that you can take a little counsel from the Lord, and feel a little of your extreme poverty and destitution...

Now reader, you need present revelation from God to your own dear self, in order to help you out of this nasty confused labyrinth, and to set your feet firmly upon the solid rock of revelation, Mere flesh and blood cannot help you now, it requires an almighty arm to effect your deliverance. Therefore, put no more trust in man, for a curse rests upon him that will be guided by the precepts of man. I do not ask you to be guided by what I say to you, unless the Lord from heaven, shall reveal to you that I speak the truth to you, in all sobriety, yet my knowing it does not suffice for you. You also must know it for yourself, and not for another. This is your right and privilege. For God has made this promise to you and not to you, reader, only, but to all others whom He calls to repentance. Now go and get revelation for yourself...

When you see also the gross beastly sexual abominations that are increasing among all nations, without shame or fear, you will not marvel that God is determined to raise up a righteous seed and glorious branch, by re-establishing the Patriarchal Order, as in the days of Aabraham, Jacob, David, Solomon, and Elkana. Neither will you marvel while the Spirit of God is upon you, that men and even women should sneer at the sacred institution of marriage being an institution wholly under the control of God, as it was in the days of Abram...

Why should you not marvel at the sneers? Because, we have been distinctly and emphatically forewarned that in the last days there shall arise scoffers, walking after their own heart's lusts, who shall speak evil of dignities and things that they know not, having men's person's in admiration because of gain...

Now there are several ways in which the pure and obedient get revelations. It will be your privilege in due time to become acquainted with these various ways. One way is, through the inspiration of the Spirit. The Spirit is given to every man to profit withal. All men have such a measure of the Holy Spirit as to enable them to make profitable use of the light and opportunities that they have, and to obey the law under which they are placed...

Now, reader, I entreat you to seek the aid of present revelations from God. You need them just as much as any poor creature ever did, that has been born into the world. Without them you never can know God, worlds without end.

The author believes that **God** has sent prophets from time to time to show His children how to maintain freedom for themselves. He believes that these have been few and far between because of the natural principle that demands of us, individual effort for our own development. Anyone can be a follower. Only those of strong character will do right on their own, without a forceful leader to guide them.

Strong individuals will be needed now for the establishment of Zion and implementation of correct civil **Law**. Probably other prophets will be raised up. If not, so what! We have ample instruction from those who've gone before. We need only to study their works and exercise our own abilities, including willingness to seek and accept guidance of the Spirit.

Most will never accept or be willing to gather with Israel. Most realize only a small portion of their own production, but are content nevertheless, with their level of survival. The author has not yet lived in abject poverty, but neither is he blind to much suffering among his people. Our present system is not providing equal opportunity for all. It does not, in fact, provide for most of us, opportunity for the security and comfort intended for us by Him who tried to give it to us all.

Hang on, if you will, to your meager subsistence and the station to which you've become accustomed. Turning into statues of salt is not predicted for those of us who can't stand to leave behind us, our way of life. Great suffering will take place, though, for you and your loved ones, if you refuse to heed this warning.

The **gathering of Israel** will be into countries to the south of Babylon. If you've read a little scripture, you understand that the lost tribes will come down out of the north. Where else then, but to the south? This does not for one minute, mean that any existing nation will become Zion. The Zion of our **God**, will be established initially as a haven of safety for Israelites, migrating southward out of Babylonian lands.

Nations unto which Israel will flee, will tolerate the establishment of a society, within their territories. Don't forget that Zion will be a law abiding society that will not threaten the nations into which she flees. A great deal of the blood of Israel already exists in the Latin American Countries. No, this is not to say that these peoples are living under just laws. All the governments on earth are, at this time, following the evil one.

The masses of the people in the southern lands are more humble and, therefore, more tolerant than we Babylonians. In any event, the author did not choose the place for the gathering. Prophets of **God** told us to come out of Babylon.[33] They told us also that we'd come down out of the North. It is acknowledged here that our **God** has a right to decide how and where he will accomplish his ends. If He wants us to go south, then those who choose to comply with his wishes will do it his way. Those who choose not to comply with his demands will not do so.

Those who choose to deny that we have a Creator are like children who deny that their earthly parents gave them birth. They can deny it to their dying day but, it will not change the facts. Whether you accept or deny your **God**, you are subject to the powers that be in this world. There are two sides only, good and evil. Neither of the individuals who head up the two protocols are visible to most of us. The deeds of their followers are plainly in view. We all can, and do, choose whom we will follow. That choice is clearly our own to make. If you choose not to take the sword up against your neighbor, you will have to come out of Babylon. The sooner you make this choice, the easier the road will be for you.

"Pray that your flight will not be in the middle of the night, *and pray ye that your flight be not in the winter.*[34] Pray that you won't be big with child and walking over the mountains in your bare feet. Those who sit back, waiting for **God** to do it all for them will find that *He helps those who help themselves.* Yes, He will help us, but He won't do it all. We must prove willingness to join his camp. We'll have to take sides in the "Coming Crisis."

The author has told the truth. These things are not dreamed up, but are in evidence all around us. Laws of **God** and nature are **eternal**. You can't change them. The author can't change them. If **God** can, He will not. The author is not a prophet, but scriptures herein quoted were given to us by prophets. The author has no special calling. He is not a priest of **God**. He understands that we all have a duty to disseminate the truth as we see it, to do good, if you will, where we can.

---

[33] Revelation 18:4
[34] Mark 13:18

Because we cherish **Liberty**, we're going to reclaim it
There's nothing that can hold us back from winning this last gambit
Because it is our **God's** design, to wind the scene up thus
We'll reestablish freedom. No power on earth can stop us
The Israelitish Nation is scattered round our sphere
But now we'll gather to a place that's free from doubt and fear
We'll listen to our Maker's call, we'll come from far and near
To build the mighty Zion and all will prosper there
Prosperity, security, are ours by right, you know
We're going to reclaim them and never let them go
A system built on justice, with fair and honest rules
Will replace Satan's myriad of governments of fools
So now it's time for Israelites to take back what we've lost
We'll now renew our promise to be honest, true and just
And give to ours, free agency, no matter what the cost

Dedicate yourself to peace. Determine not to take the sword up against your neighbor or your brother. Stay out of the fray. Gather with Israel to Zion. Join with us and help us to establish the **City of Liberty and Peace**.

This work closes appropriately with the words of the Lord **God** through the prophet Jeremiah:

Jeremiah 16:15 *But, The Lord liveth, that brought up the children of Israel from the land of the north, and from all the lands whither he had driven them: and I will bring them again into their land that I gave unto their fathers.*

Jeremiah 30:24 *The fierce anger of the Lord shall not return, until he have done it, and until he have performed the intents of his heart: in the latter days ye shall consider it.*

Jeremiah 31:1-14 *At the same time, saith the Lord, will I be the God of all the families of Israel, and they shall be my people, 2 Thus saith the Lord, The people which were left of the sword found grace in the wilderness; even Israel, and they shall be my people. 3 The Lord hath appeared of old unto me, saying, Yea, I have thee with an ever-lasting love: therefore with loving kindness have I drawn thee. 4 Again I will build thee, and thou shalt be built, O virgin of Israel: thou shalt again be adorned with thy tabrets, and shalt go forth in the dances of them that make merry. 5 Thou shalt yet plant vines upon the mountains of Samaria: the planters shall plant, and shall eat them as common things. 6 For there shall be a day, that the watchman upon the mount Ephraim shall cry, Arise ye, and let us go up to Zion unto the Lord our God. 7 For thus saith the Lord; Sing with gladness for Jacob, and shout among the chief of the nations: publish ye, praise ye and say, O Lord, save thy people, the remnant of Israel. 8 Behold, I will bring them from the north country and gather them from the coasts of the earth, and with them the blind and the lame, the woman with child and her that travaileth with child together: a great company shall return thither. 9 They shall come with weeping, and with supplications will I lead them: I will cause them to walk by the rivers of waters in a straight way, wherein they shall not stumble: for I am a father to Israel, and Ephraim is my firstborn. 10 Hear the word of the Lord, O ye nations, and declare it in the isles afar off, and say, He that scattered Israel will gather him, and keep him, as a shepherd doth his flock. 11 For the Lord hath redeemed Jacob, and ransomed him from the hand of him that was stronger than he. 12 Therefore they shall come and sing in the height of Zion, and shall flow together to the goodness of the Lord, for wheat, and for wine, and for oil, and for the young of the flock and of the herd: and their soul shall be as a watered garden; and they shall not sorrow any more at all 13 Then shall the virgin rejoice in the dance, both young men and old together: for I will turn their mourning into joy, and will comfort them, and make them rejoice from their sorrow. 14 And I will satiate the soul of the priests with fatness, and my people shall be satisfied with my goodness, saith the Lord.*

ABOUT THE AUTHOR

Born in Mpls Minnesota in 1938. Mr. Shrewsbury was raised in Minnesota and Utah and lived in the northern states, southern states, eastern states , western states and the Mid west. He served a short term of active military service (honorably discharged). He spent four years in Guatemala during the time President Idigores was ousted from power through a military coupe.

Mr. Shrewsbury spent approximately five years in Mexico in short bursts. In the early nineties was tried in federal court on five counts of violations of the EPA regulations and was found not guilty on all charges. Building contractor with experience in mining, logging and electro plating.

He raised a family and is currently alone. He has six children scattered throughout the USA.

www.ingramcontent.com/pod-product-compliance
Lightning Source LLC
Chambersburg PA
CBHW020418290526
45785CB00002B/616